D0940054

Library Basics Series

1. *Learn Library of Congress Classification,* Helena Dittmann and Jane Hardy, 2000
2. *Learn Dewey Decimal Classification (Edition 21),* Mary Mortimer, 2000
3. *Learn Descriptive Cataloging,* Mary Mortimer, 2000
4. *Learn Library of Congress Subject Access,* Jacki Ganendran, 2000
5. *Learn Basic Library Skills,* Elaine Andersen, Mary Gosling, and Mary Mortimer; North American editors: Mary McConnell and Trina Grover, 2002

NORTHEAST COMMUNITY COLLEGE LIBRARY

WITHDRAWN

NORTHEAST COMMUNITY COLLEGE LIBRARY

Learn Basic Library Skills

Elaine Andersen
Mary Gosling
Mary Mortimer

North American Editors
Mary McConnell
Trina Grover

Library Basics, No. 5

The Scarecrow Press, Inc.
Lanham, Maryland, and Oxford
in cooperation with
DocMatrix Pty Ltd, Canberra, Australia
2002

020
A5441

SCARECROW PRESS, INC.

Published in the United States of America
by Scarecrow Press, Inc.
A Member of the Rowman & Littlefield Publishing Group
4720 Boston Way, Lanham, Maryland 20706
www.scarecrowpress.com

PO Box 317
Oxford
OX2 9RU, UK

Copyright © 2002 by DocMatrix Pty Ltd
This 1st North American edition is based on Elaine Andersen, Mary Gosling, Mary Mortimer/
Learn Basic Library Skills/DocMatrix Pty Ltd/1998, to which has been added new and updated material.

All rights reserved. No part of this publication may be reproduced, stored in a retrieval system,
or transmitted in any form or by any means, electronic, mechanical, photocopying, recording,
or otherwise, without the prior permission of the publisher.

Design by Andrew Rankine Design Associates pty ltd, Canberra, Australia

British Library and National Library of Australia Cataloguing in Publication Information Available

Library of Congress Cataloging-in-Publication Data
Andersen, Elaine, 1951–
   Learn basic library skills / Elaine Andersen, Mary Gosling, Mary Mortimer.—North American ed. /
edited by Mary McConnell, Trina Grover.
     p. cm. — (Library basics series ; 5)
  Includes bibliographical references and index.
  ISBN 0-8108-4498-2 (alk. paper)
   1. Library science. I. Gosling, Mary, 1951– II. Mortimer, Mary, 1944– III. McConnell, Mary
(Mary Eleanor) IV. Grover, Trina. V. Title. VI. Series.
Z665 .A56 2002
020–dc21   2002026811

♾™The paper used in this publication meets the minimum requirements of American National
Standard for Information Sciences—Permanence of Paper for Printed Library Materials,
ANSI/NISO Z39.48–1992. Manufactured in the United States of America.

CONTENTS

PREFACE

Learn basic library skills describes the skills needed by anyone beginning work in a library or other information agency, whether at a professional or a paraprofessional level. The book explains tasks usually allotted to staff who "begin at the bottom": clerical, temporary, casual, and volunteer staff; library trainees; aspiring library technicians; librarians starting their training; and others who begin work in a library with no relevant education or experience. The book is designed for use on its own or in a formal course of study.

Each chapter deals with a section of basic library work and the knowledge and skills needed to perform it well. The more you understand the tasks and procedures and the reasons for doing them, the more competently you will be able to carry them out.

Where standard rules exist (e.g., filing rules), they are included. For procedures that vary from library to library, we outline common approaches or encourage you to find out how it is done in a library you know.

Throughout the book, you will find exercises to practice your skills and quizzes to test your understanding. There are answers for self-checking provided at the back of the book. We suggest that, whenever possible, you discuss the questions and issues with experienced library staff and/or your course instructors. We are aware that you may not have access to all of the library facilities and bibliographic tools suggested in the exercises, so we have tried to include a variety of exercises to allow for this situation.

Libraries are great places to work if the work suits you; if not, you risk conflicting endlessly with the rules and doing an unsatisfactory job as well. If, having read this introduction, you are not sure that library work is for you, talk to someone (e.g., teacher, supervisor, librarian, informed friend) about your choice. If, on the other hand, you can't wait to get started, we hope you enjoy it.

ACKNOWLEDGMENTS

Thanks to Nancy Ritchie, Rob McConnell, Aileen Farray, Ursula Nocon, and Natalie Briggs for their assistance.

Chapter 1
BASIC LIBRARY SKILLS

Introduction

The purpose of libraries is to connect people with the information they want. To achieve this purpose, library staff need:

- reliable and consistent access to information
- communication skills
- technical skills to organize and access the information.

Information

Traditionally, information has been collected in libraries. Although this is still largely the case, libraries now obtain more and more information, or enable clients to find the information they need, from other sources. Interlibrary loan and document delivery, discussed in Chapter 3, explain how libraries use outside sources to expand their information services.

Physical Formats of Library Material

Information is packaged in many physical formats. Most users are not concerned about the form in which the information is presented, provided it is easily accessible. Sometimes, however, a particular format is as important as the content. For example, only an audiocassette will meet the need of someone who travels long distances in a car with an audiocassette player.

Libraries usually group materials into a number of physical formats to manage them more easily.

Print Materials

Monographs

Monograph means "produced once" and is derived from *mono* (Latin for *one*) and *graph* (Greek for *write*). The term is generally used to describe printed books in order to distinguish them from serials (see below).

Print monographs include:

printed books: sheets of paper generally printed on both sides, folded and sewn, glued or spiral bound, enclosed in a cover

manuscripts: usually on paper, written by hand (e.g., drafts of novels or poems)

typescripts: similar to manuscripts, but produced on a typewriter

pamphlets: unbound works of less than 50 pages

ephemera: printed material intended to have a short life (e.g., leaflets, sale catalogs, political pamphlets, menus, theater programs)

computer printouts: similar to typescripts but produced by a printer linked to a computer

newspaper clippings: news items, articles, etc., cut from newspapers, indexed, and filed.

Serials

Print serials are also called periodicals. They include journals, magazines, newspapers, and annuals. They are publications that are issued at regular or irregular intervals, have a common title, and are intended to continue indefinitely.

Monographs in Series

Some monographs are published as part of a series. Many libraries treat these as monographs, acquiring and cataloging each item separately as it arrives. Some libraries, however, require every title in a series and arrange with the vendor to ensure that each title is forwarded to the library when it is published. These books are bought, processed, and recorded within the serials subsystem by serials staff. This arrangement is often referred to as a **standing order**.

Non-Print Materials

This category also contains monographs and serials and is usually referred to as non-book material. The procedures for ordering and receiving this type of material often match those used to acquire print monographs and serials, but it is common practice to subdivide the material into smaller categories that share similar physical characteristics.

These categories include:
maps, plans, diagrams: large sheets, usually of paper or card stock, with cartographic or diagrammatic information; generally intended to be folded, rolled, or hung

pictures: single sheets on which pictorial information is displayed (e.g., drawings, paintings, prints, photographs)

microform: documents reproduced in miniature for economy of storage and weight; read by projecting the enlarged image onto a screen (e.g., microfilm, microfiche)

films and slides: photographic images developed frame by frame onto a strip of cellulose

videotape: magnetic tape with visual and audio recordings

sound recording: vinyl records, audiocassettes, compact discs

computer software: electronically stored information on floppy disks or CD-ROMs; accessed by computer

artifacts, realia: real, hand-made, or machine-made three-dimensional objects.

Serials

Non-book serials are packaged in the formats listed above. Although a CD-ROM serial physically resembles other CD-ROMs, it may require different treatment when it is ordered and received by the library.

Electronic Information

Electronic information—information accessed by means of a computer—is available in several forms. It includes information packaged on computer discs and tapes (e.g., floppy discs and CD-ROMs, as listed above). This material can be used in the library (provided the appropriate computer hardware is available). In some libraries, clients can also borrow computer files and software in the same way they borrow other library material.

Information is also increasingly available online—that is, accessed by computer but not physically stored in the library. The Internet, a network of networks that connects computers, allows people to search online catalogs and electronic databases all over the world. Some of these contain the whole text of articles, and even complete books, that can be read online, printed out, or copied onto a computer disc. Other databases just provide basic information about the item (e.g., author, title of the article, title of the journal, issue of the journal). Clients use this information to find the item in the library's collection, in another library's collection, or via a computer.

In dealing with electronic information, the traditional distinction between monographs and serials is no longer as clear-cut. A document available on the Internet, accompanied by an invitation to other readers to alter it, may be changed many times and soon will appear to be very different from the original. Is it a monograph, a serial, or something else for which there is not yet a category?

Leading library thinkers are just beginning to grapple with these issues. We will not attempt to deal with them except to signal that developments in electronic information are challenging many traditional library concepts and procedures.

Communication Skills

Being able to communicate effectively is a basic requirement of working in any information agency. Every aspect of the work—from identifying exactly what clients want to locating and providing the information—requires good communication skills.

In particular, library staff need to be able to:
- make clients feel welcome and comfortable
- find out exactly what clients wish to know
- teach clients to find information themselves
- work as a team with other staff members
- liaise with other information agencies
- consult with professional colleagues
- communicate information
- help clients to pursue other sources of information.

Basic Organization of a Library

Libraries are organized to store information so that clients and staff can retrieve it in the most effective manner. There are, however, many variations in how libraries organize their staff to carry out this goal. In this introduction we describe the most traditional functional design of a library staff structure. (For a discussion of this and other structures, see Bob Pymm's *Learn library management*, from which the following diagram is adapted.)

Functional Design

This structure usually consists of a number of sections that deal with library materials and services. Although the diagram includes the functions of administration and information technology, the description that follows focuses on the sections of technical services and public services.

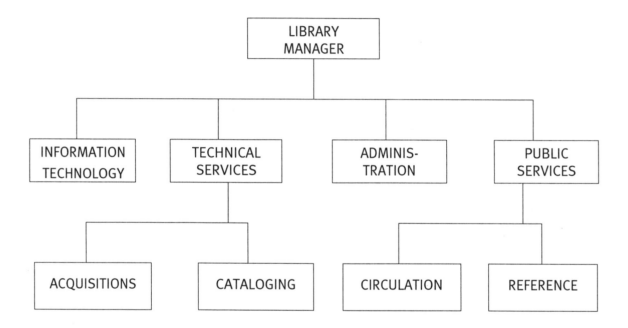

As shown above, technical services acquire and organize material. Duties include receiving and processing the material (e.g., acquisition, cataloging, and collection maintenance). Large libraries often also include sections that deal with particular formats (e.g., serials or music).

In contrast, public services deal directly with the needs of clients. These services include borrowing and returning materials, shelving, answering users' enquiries, and library instruction.

Each of these two sections has its own set of tasks that require particular knowledge and skills, but they need to liaise with each other and with the other sections of the library.

Workflow

The following diagram (adapted from Gosling & Hopgood, *Learn about information*) illustrates a typical workflow in a library. It is followed by a description of the work of each section.

Flow of Material through a Library

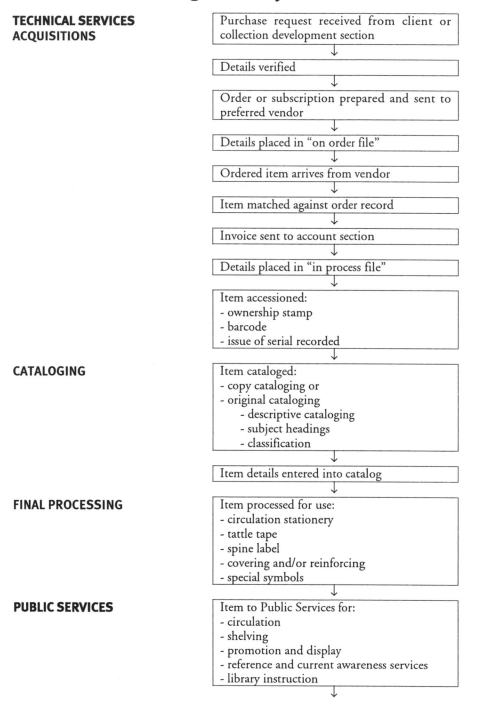

TECHNICAL SERVICES
ACQUISITIONS

Purchase request received from client or collection development section
↓
Details verified
↓
Order or subscription prepared and sent to preferred vendor
↓
Details placed in "on order file"
↓
Ordered item arrives from vendor
↓
Item matched against order record
↓
Invoice sent to account section
↓
Details placed in "in process file"
↓
Item accessioned:
- ownership stamp
- barcode
- issue of serial recorded
↓

CATALOGING

Item cataloged:
- copy cataloging or
- original cataloging
    - descriptive cataloging
    - subject headings
    - classification
↓
Item details entered into catalog
↓

FINAL PROCESSING

Item processed for use:
- circulation stationery
- tattle tape
- spine label
- covering and/or reinforcing
- special symbols
↓

PUBLIC SERVICES

Item to Public Services for:
- circulation
- shelving
- promotion and display
- reference and current awareness services
- library instruction
↓

Flow of Material through a Library (cont.)

**COLLECTION
MAINTENANCE**

Ongoing collection maintenance, either in
Technical Services or Public Services:
- shelving and shelf-reading
- repair
- inventory
- weeding
- discarding
- binding

Technical Services

Acquisitions

This section acquires new material for the library's collection. Tasks include ordering, receiving, checking that incoming materials match the order, arranging for payment, marking the library's ownership, and recording receipt of all new library material. It may also include receiving (sometimes even soliciting) gifts and exchanges and deciding how to handle them. The financial responsibility requires keeping track of the library's spending and knowing when and if the money may run out, how much funding remains, and whether the library is within its budget allocation.

Cataloging

This section maintains **bibliographic control** of the library's collection. That is, the staff create records that describe items, assign classification numbers and subject headings, and record these details in the catalog and, sometimes, in authority files.

The preliminary work of this section requires searching of the library's (and often other) catalogs and databases to find existing records for the items or records that assist the library staff in creating original ones.

Although automated systems have reduced the amount of filing done by library staff, there are still libraries with manual circulation systems and/or catalogs where cards need to be filed. Even if computers file the records, library staff need to know how this process is done in order to find them again.

Final Processing

After items have been cataloged, they are prepared for loan and/or use in the library. This involves labeling: the call number is placed on the spine of each book or indicated clearly on other types of material. Some libraries cover and/or otherwise strengthen books to prolong their lives. Non-book material is packaged so that it can be shelved and borrowed easily. Any stationery needed for circulation (e.g., date due slips) or security (e.g., tattle tape) is added at this stage.

Public Services

Circulation

The lending and returning of library materials are key services. To do this, staff must understand the intricacies of the circulation system whether it is manual or automated. It is also necessary to know how to deal with the library's clients, especially if they are impatient or dissatisfied with the service.

Shelving

Items must be shelved correctly so that clients can find them. Staff should check the shelves regularly to ensure that items have been replaced accurately.

Promotion and Display

It is important for the library to promote its services to all of its potential clients so that it is regularly used and its value appreciated. Promotional activities range from running an art competition during Book Week to offering specialized current awareness programs within an organization; from displaying new acquisitions on shelves in the library foyer to emailing individual clients to notify them of items of particular interest.

Reference and Current Awareness Service

Reference services vary considerably among libraries depending on the nature and purpose of the library and the level of staff assigned to this section. For example, in a corporate or legislative library, services can include providing answers to specific questions, performing extensive searches, and recording the results. In a public or school library, services could focus on maintaining a good reference collection and assisting clients in finding the information themselves.

Library Instruction

Libraries are used more effectively by clients who understand the library's organization and its methods of locating information. Staff can provide assistance ranging from one-on-one instruction to teaching groups how to use the catalog, find answers to specific questions, access information on the Internet, and so on.

As more information is retrieved electronically, especially via the Internet, it becomes increasingly important to teach clients to define their information needs, to identify the most likely sources, and to evaluate the results.

It is vital for library staff to "add value" to sources of information such as the Internet, CD-ROMs, and so forth so that clients benefit from their information retrieval skills. Unless library staff promote their skills in these areas, the community may conclude that libraries and their specialist staff are no longer relevant to the process of obtaining information.

Collection Maintenance

This encompasses the activities involved in keeping the collection current, attractive, and easy to use. Activities include shelving and shelf-reading, repair of damaged items, inventory, and weeding. Public services staff perform several of the tasks, technical services staff are responsible for others, and both sections may work together on some activities.

Technical Skills

Technical skills are needed to organize library material. Accuracy and attention to detail are the basis of strong technical skills in library work.

Libraries, even small ones, store a great deal of material. Staff need to be able to find items quickly. This requires creating consistent records and maintaining them accurately to prevent problems.

Examples of problems include:

- The incorrect spelling of an author's name prevents a book from being found easily.
- Clients are irritated if they receive overdue notices because returned items were not properly discharged.
- Hours can be wasted searching for a "missing" issue of a serial that has been put in the wrong box.

Over the years, libraries have developed rules and procedures to streamline their work and provide a reliable information environment. With the advent of automation, libraries can share the records they create and reduce the amount of work formerly done at each site. With improved telecommunications, clients can access information stored in remote locations. These added benefits demand that the procedures used for the recording and storing of information provide consistency. Only then will the processes become simpler rather than more complex.

Some standards used in libraries are international. At higher levels of library work, items are cataloged using *Anglo-American cataloguing rules, MARC formats, Library of Congress* or *Dewey decimal classification,* and *Library of Congress subject headings.* In automated library systems, Z39.50 standards are now widely used and specialists are developing additional standards for describing online data.

At a more basic level, there are standard procedures for many of the tasks described in this book. In acquisitions sections, libraries record a standard set of details—author, title, edition, date of publication, and so on—to identify the items they order. With the help of automated library systems, catalogers can access these entries and create catalog records using the same basic information.

Records must be filed using established filing rules, or the task of finding them becomes more difficult. Similarly, items are shelved using standard procedures so that clients and library staff can locate them easily.

In addition to the standard rules and procedures, each library has its own methods of performing some tasks. These methods arise from (among other things):

- the library's history: "We've always done it like that."
- the needs of clients: "Our managing director insists on being first to see the new journals."
- the peculiarities of the library's system: "It seems to work faster if you scan the item's barcode first."

Chapter 2
BIBLIOGRAPHIC RECORDS

Introduction
Libraries contain large numbers of items that must be found whenever the information they contain is needed. Methods of organization include:

- arranging items on shelves according to subject and/or author or title
- describing each item, including its subject(s), and providing these details in a library catalog
- listing items in a bibliography that is made available to interested people
- adding information about the items to databases maintained outside the library (e.g., contributing your library holdings to union catalogs)
- amalgamating details of separate library collections to make them accessible to clients of other libraries and information services
- analyzing the content of items and publishing the details of parts of items (e.g., articles in a periodical) either in printed or electronic form.

Keeping track of all the items in a collection, and recording them in such a way that they can be found when needed, is called **bibliographic control.** Most of the methods of bibliographic control listed above require the creation of bibliographic records.

What Is a Bibliographic Record?
A bibliographic record is an entry in card, print, microform, machine-readable, or any other form that contains bibliographic information about a given item.

The bibliographic record represents the item. It allows the details of a large number of items to be contained in a searchable tool (e.g., book, periodical, CD-ROM, online database) and enables searchers to find items that contain the information they need.

A bibliographic record usually includes:
- a description of the item
- information about the content (subject) of the item
- headings or access points

and sometimes:
- details of its location.

The description helps searchers decide whether the item is the one they require or whether it contains the information they want. The content may be described in words taken from the item or from a special list of terms and/or numbers that represent subjects. The access points help to find information about a particular item or group of items. The location information helps to locate the physical item.

Standardizing Bibliographic Records

The more bibliographic records are exchanged, and the more sources of information library clients can now access, the more important it has become to standardize these records. Standard bibliographic descriptions allow libraries to share records that contain the same details and are arranged in the same way. Similarly, it is much easier for users of the records to deal with one standard format containing elements that are recognizable and reliable.

For many decades, libraries have standardized their records—especially catalog records. We will look first at some of the rules for creating standard catalog records so you can recognize the information contained in them and the way in which they are arranged. Full cataloging procedures are not dealt with in this book because they are more complex than required at this level and need to be studied separately. Workbooks that treat descriptive cataloging, subject headings, and classification are also available in the Library Basics series.

The same principles apply in many other works and databases that contain bibliographic records (called bibliographic tools), although there are also differences in arrangement and amount of detail. You need to familiarize yourself with the basic bibliographic tools used in most libraries and with the specialized tools for your library or subject field as well. Chapter 5 discusses some common bibliographic tools (apart from the catalog).

Elements of Bibliographic Records

A bibliographic record consists of many elements: author(s), title, publisher, date of publication, and so on. Since these identify the item, most standard elements are common to all bibliographic records.

Most library collections consist of works in a variety of formats, such as monographs, serials, audiovisual materials, manuscripts, photographs, and computer files. In addition to the common bibliographic elements, different formats require some different bibliographic elements to describe and identify particular items.

A Catalog Card Record of a Monograph

```
                                                    305.42
                                                    GRE
Greer, Germaine, 1939-

The madwoman's underclothes : essays and occasional writings /
Germaine Greer. – 1st American ed. – New York : Atlantic
Monthly Press, 1987, c1986.
xxvii, 305 p. ; 24 cm.
ISBN 0871131609.

1. Greer, Germaine, 1939-    . 2. Feminists – Biography.
3. Feminism. 4. Social history – 1945-    . I. Title.
```

A Book Catalog Record of a Serial

025.2/1
Library collections, acquisitions & technical services. Vol. 23,
no. 1 (spring 1999)-   . – New York : Pergamon, c1999-   . -
v. : ill. ; 26 cm.
ISSN 1464-9055 = Library collections, acquisitions & technical
services.
Quarterly.
Continues: Library acquisitions, practice and theory =   ISSN
0364-6408.
Subjects: Acquisitions (Libraries) – Periodicals.   Collection
management (Libraries) – Periodicals. Processing (Libraries) –
Periodicals.

An Online Catalog Record of a Monograph

TITLE	The wisdom of teams : creating the high-performance organization / Jon R. Katzenbach, Douglas K. Smith.
AUTHOR	Katzenbach, Jon R., 1932-
ADD AUTHOR	Smith, Douglas K., 1949-
EDITION	1st HarperBusiness ed.
PUBLISHER	New York, N.Y. : HarperBusiness, 1994.
ISBN/ISSN	0-887-30676-4.
PHYS DESCR	xii, 317 p. : ill. ; 21 cm.
SUBJECT	Teams in the workplace.
NOTE	Originally published: Boston, Mass. : Harvard Business School Press, 1993 Includes bibliographical references (p. 301-303) and index.
CALL NUMBER	658.3/128

An Online Catalog Record of a Videorecording

CALL NUMBER	Videocass 005459
TITLE	42 up [videorecording].
PUBLISHER	[Great Britain] : Granada Television, 1998.
DESCRIPT'N	1 videocassette (VHS) (130 min.) : sd., col. ; 1/2 in.
SUMMARY	Continues the 7-up series in which a group of English men and women are revisited at seven year intervals to chart their progress through life. Of the original 14 subjects, 11 remain.
SUBJECT	1) Children—Great Britain—Longitudinal studies. 2) Great Britain—Social studies.
AUTHOR(S)	1) Apted, Michael.
ORGANIZ'N	Granada Television.

An Example

Here is some of the information about a book. The bibliographic record represents this book by including the elements used to identify it. The main information is taken from the title page and the verso of the title page. Information is also taken from other parts of the item and sometimes from sources other than the item itself.

Title page

Newmarket Shooting Script Series

SNOW FALLING ON CEDARS

Screenplay by
Ron Bass and Scott Hicks

Based on the novel by
David Guterson

Commentaries by
Scott Hicks and Kathleen Kennedy

NEWMARKET PRESS – NEW YORK

Title page verso

Design and compilation copyright © 1999 by Newmarket Press. All rights reserved.

This book is published simultaneously in the United States of America and in Canada.

First Edition

ISBN 1-55704-372-8 (pb)

This book has 166 pages with illustrations. It is 24 cm. high.

The most important information about this book appears in the following worksheet. It contains a description of the book and the headings under which a client may look for it.

Title	Snow Falling on Cedars
Authors, editors, compilers, translators, illustrators, etc.	Ron Bass, Scott Hicks, Kathleen Kennedy
Edition (if any)	1st
Place(s) of publication	New York
Name of publisher(s)	Newmarket Press
Date of publication	1999
Physical description	166 pages, illustrations, 24 cm.
Series (if any)	Newmarket Shooting Script Series
Notes (i.e., any other information you think could help to find or identify the item)	Based on the novel by David Guterson
Numbers (ISBN, ISSN, other relevant numbers)	ISBN 1-55704-372-8

EXERCISE 2.1

Here are some title pages and title page versos. Complete a worksheet for each, noting all the elements that you think may help a library client to identify the work or that may be useful access points into a catalog or index. Not every item will contain all the bibliographic elements. <u>You are not cataloging the items</u>; just copy information you think is relevant.

a.   Series title page

FORGOTTEN REALMS
Fantasy Adventure

Title page

ONCE AROUND THE REALMS
A Picaresque Romp

Brian M. Thomsen

TSR

Title page verso

ONCE AROUND THE REALMS

© 1995 TSR, Inc.
All Rights Reserved

First Printing: April 1995
Printed in the United States of America
Library of Congress Catalog Card Number: 94-68134

ISBN: 0-7869-0119-5

TSR, Inc.   TSR Ltd.
201 Sheridan Springs Rd.   120 Church End, Cherry Hinton
Lake Geneva, WI 53147   Cambridge CB1 3LB
U.S.A.   United Kingdom

This book has 307 pages and illustrations. It is 18 cm. high.

Title	
Authors, editors, compilers, translators, illustrators, etc.	
Edition (if any)	
Place(s) of publication	
Name of publisher(s)	
Date of publication	
Physical description	
Series (if any)	
Notes (i.e., any other information you think could help to find or identify the item)	
Numbers (ISBN, ISSN, other relevant numbers)	

b.   Title page

BDK English Tripitaka 10-I

THE STOREHOUSE OF
SUNDRY VALUABLES

Translated from the Chinese of Kikkaya
and Liu Hsiao-piao (Compiled by T'an-yao)

by Charles Willemen

Numata Center
for Buddhist Translation and Research
1994

Title page verso

© 1994 by Bukkyo Dendo Kyokai and Numata Center
for Buddhist Translation and Research

First Printing, 1994
ISBN: 0-9625618-3-5
Library of Congress Catalog Card Number: 92-082068

Published by
Numata Center for Buddhist Translation and Research
2620 Warring Street
Berkeley, California 94704

Printed in the United States of America

This book is in English and Chinese, has 275 pages, bibliographical references, and an index. There are no illustrations. It is 23.5 cm. high.

Title	
Authors, editors, compilers, translators, illustrators, etc.	
Edition (if any)	
Place(s) of publication	
Name of publisher(s)	
Date of publication	
Physical description	
Series (if any)	
Notes (i.e., any other information you think could help to find or identify the item)	
Numbers (ISBN, ISSN, other relevant numbers)	

c. Title page

EVERYTHING YOU
ALWAYS WANTED TO
KNOW ABOUT SEX*

**Explained by
David R. Reuben, M.D.**

*BUT WERE AFRAID TO ASK

BANTAM BOOKS
TORONTO • NEW YORK • LONDON

Title page verso

EVERYTHING YOU ALWAYS WANTED TO
KNOW ABOUT SEX
*A Bantam Book / published by arrangement with
David McKay Company, Inc.*

PRINTING HISTORY
McKay edition published November 1969

2nd printing	*December 1969*	*10th printing*	*March 1970*
3rd printing	*January 1970*	*11th printing*	*March 1970*
4th printing	*January 1970*	*12th printing*	*March 1970*
5th printing	*January 1970*	*13th printing*	*April 1970*
6th printing	*February 1970*	*14th printing*	*April 1970*
7th printing	*February 1970*	*15th printing*	*May 1970*
8th printing	*February 1970*	*16th printing*	*May 1970*
9th printing	*February 1970*	*17th printing*	*June 1970*

18th printing   July 1970
Book Find Club edition published May 1970
Book-of-the-Month Club edition published June 1970
Psychology Today edition published May 1970
Bantam edition published January 1971

All rights reserved.
Copyright © 1969 by David R. Reuben, M.D.

This book has 433 pages and an index. There are no illustrations. It is 18 cm. high.

Title	
Authors, editors, compilers, translators, illustrators, etc.	
Edition (if any)	
Place(s) of publication	
Name of publisher(s)	
Date of publication	
Physical description	
Series (if any)	
Notes (i.e., any other information you think could help to find or identify the item)	
Numbers (ISBN, ISSN, other relevant numbers)	

d.   Cover

Blandford Colour Series
**Balloons and
Airships**

Lennart Ege

Title page

The Pocket Encyclopaedia
of World Aircraft in Colour

BALLOONS AND
AIRSHIPS
1783-1983

by
LENNART EGE

Editor of the English edition
KENNETH MUNSON
from translation prepared by
ERIK HILDESHEIM

Illustrated by
OTTO FRELLO

LONDON
BLANDFORD PRESS

Title page verso

First English edition 1983
Reprinted 1984

English text © Blandford Press Ltd
167 High Holborn, London WC1V 6PH

ISBN 0 7137 0568 X

This book has 234 pages, color illustrations, black-and-white illustrations, and an index. It is 18.5 cm. high.

Title	
Authors, editors, compilers, translators, illustrators, etc.	
Edition (if any)	
Place(s) of publication	
Name of publisher(s)	
Date of publication	
Physical description	
Series (if any)	
Notes (i.e., any other information you think could help to find or identify the item)	
Numbers (ISBN, ISSN, other relevant numbers)	

International Standard Bibliographic Description (ISBD)

Catalog records form the basis of the bibliographic control of most libraries. Items in the library's collection are described using the International Standard Bibliographic Description (ISBD) developed by the International Federation of Library Associations and Institutions (IFLA). This is the standard used in the *Anglo-American cataloguing rules second edition (AACR2)*.

The ISBD:
- lists all the elements required to describe and identify all types of material
- assigns an order to those elements
- prescribes punctuation for those elements.

Areas of Description

The description is divided into eight areas:
- title and statement of responsibility
- edition
- material (or type of publication) specific details
- publication, distribution, etc.
- physical description
- series
- note
- standard number and terms of availability.

Some items require all areas of description. Most items, however, do not need all of them. In these cases, the description includes only the appropriate areas.

An Example

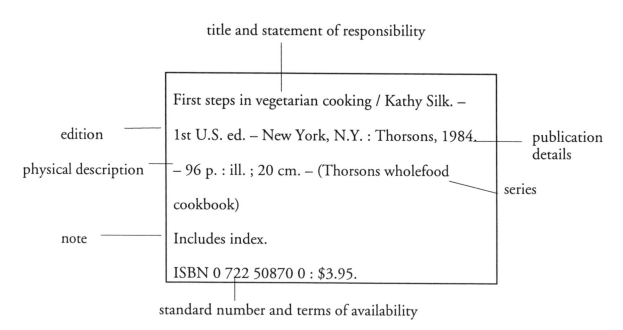

EXERCISE 2.2

In each of the following descriptions, highlight and name each of the areas.

a.

Ben Jonson revised / Claude J. Summers and Ted-Larry Pebworth. – Rev. ed. – New York, N.Y. : Twayne Publishers, c1999. – xix, 293 p. : port. ; 23 cm. – (Twayne's English authors series ; TEAS 557)
Includes bibliographical references (p. 274-281) and index.
ISBN 0-805-77062-3.

b.

Crisis & renewal : meeting the challenge of organizational change / David K. Hurst. – Boston, Mass. : Harvard Business School Press, 1995. – xiii, 229 p. : ill. ; 25 cm. – (The management of innovation and change series)
Includes bibliographical references (p. 198-213) and indexes.
ISBN 0-875-84582-7.

c.

The Cambridge illustrated history of ancient Greece / Paul Cartledge. – Cambridge, U.K. ; New York, N.Y. : Cambridge University Press, 1998. – xix, 380 p. : ill. (some col.), maps (some col.) ; 26 cm. – (Cambridge illustrated history)
Includes bibliographical references (p. [371]-373) and index.
ISBN 0-521-48196-1.

d.

> Psychic voyages / by the editors of Time-Life Books.
> – Alexandria, Va. : Time-Life Books, c1987. – 144 p. :
> ill. (some col.) ; 28 cm. – (Mysteries of the unknown)
> Bibliography: p. 138-140.
> Includes index.
> ISBN 0-809-46316-4.

Elements of Description

Each area of the description contains a number of elements. The following outline includes most of the elements possible in the description of a monograph and the associated punctuation:

Title proper = Parallel title : other title information / first statement of responsibility ; each subsequent statement of responsibility. - Edition statement / statement of responsibility relating to the edition. - First place of publication ; second place of publication : publisher, date of publication. - Pagination : illustration ; dimensions + accompanying material. - (Title proper of series / statement of responsibility relating to series, ISSN of series ; numbering within the series) Note(s).
ISBN : price.

An Example

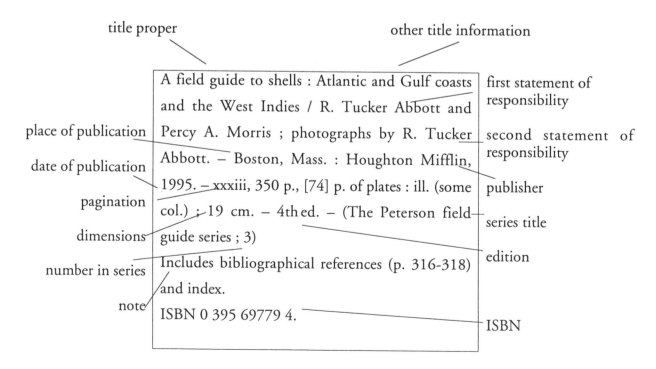

> title proper   other title information
>
> place of publication   first statement of responsibility
> date of publication   second statement of responsibility
> pagination   publisher
> dimensions   series title
> number in series   edition
> note   ISBN

A field guide to shells : Atlantic and Gulf coasts and the West Indies / R. Tucker Abbott and Percy A. Morris ; photographs by R. Tucker Abbott. – Boston, Mass. : Houghton Mifflin, 1995. – xxxiii, 350 p., [74] p. of plates : ill. (some col.) ; 19 cm. – 4th ed. – (The Peterson field guide series ; 3)
Includes bibliographical references (p. 316-318) and index.
ISBN 0 395 69779 4.

Punctuation in ISBD

ISBD uses punctuation:

- to show the beginning of each area
- to separate the elements within each area
- to identify particular elements by the punctuation that precedes them.

Punctuation precedes (or comes before) each area or element within an area. Thus, size is always preceded by a semicolon (;), no matter what else is in the physical description. For example:
xi, 309 p. : ill. ; 23 cm.
665 p. ; 21 cm.

Each area is separated by a full stop, space, dash, space, or a new line. Notes are often given separate paragraphs for readability.

Look again at the outline above of the description of a monograph and note the punctuation that introduces each of the elements. Note also that we follow the practice outlined in *Cataloging service bulletin no. 44*. This means including areas 1-6 in a single paragraph, beginning each note and the ISBN on a new line, and ending each note and the ISBN with a full stop.

Punctuation Marks

Here is a list of punctuation marks used in ISBD:

.	full stop
,	comma
:	colon
;	semicolon
-	hyphen
–	dash
/	(diagonal) slash
[ ]	square brackets
( )	parentheses
...	marks of omission (NB only 3 dots)
?	question mark
=	equals sign
+	plus sign.

EXERCISE 2.3

In each of the following records, be sure that you can identify each element. Then transcribe (i.e., write out) the particular information requested, copying the punctuation and capitalization exactly.

a. Hawaiian music and musicians : an illustrated history /

George S. Kanahele. – Honolulu : University Press of

Hawaii, c1979. – xxx, 543 p. : ill. ; 25 cm.

Bibliography: p. [503]–519.

Includes discographies and index.

ISBN 0-824-80578-X : $25.00.

Transcribe the whole title and statement of responsibility area. Underline the statement of responsibility.

b. Australia : diario di un emigrante / Sergio Trabalza. –

Trento, Italy : Scuole Grafiche Artigianelli, 1976.

236 p. : 1 map ; 21 cm.

Bibliography: p. 230.

Includes index.

Underline the title proper. Does this entry have other title information? If so, transcribe it including the punctuation that precedes it.

What is the underlined element?

c.   Planned urban environments : Sweden, Finland, Israel, the

Netherlands, France / by Ann Louise Strong. – Baltimore :

Johns Hopkins Press, 1971. - xxxiv, 406 p. : ill. ; 29 cm.

<u>Bibliography: p. 391-396.</u>

Includes index.

ISBN 0-80181-245-3.

Transcribe the whole physical description area including the punctuation that precedes it.

What is the underlined element?

d.   Education in Canada : a bibliography = L'éducation au

Canada : une bibliographie / E.G. Finley. – Toronto :

Dundern Press, 1989. – 2 v. ; 29 cm.

Text in English and French.

Includes indexes.

Transcribe the whole title and statement of responsibility area. Underline the parallel title. What is a parallel title?

EXERCISE 2.4

Write out each of the following bibliographical records using ISBD arrangement. Retain the punctuation supplied. Remember that punctuation precedes each element and area.

a.

First statement of responsibility	/ edited by Luc Sante and Melissa Holbrook Pierson
Publication, distribution, etc.	– New York : Pantheon Books, c1999
Title proper	O.K. you mugs
Physical description	. – xvi, 284 p. : ill. ; 20 cm.
ISBN	ISBN 0-37540-101-6.
Edition	. – 1st ed.
Note	Includes index.
Other title information	: writers on movie actors

b.

Title proper	Exploration, conservation, preservation
Pagination	. – xiii, 391 p.
Date	, c1999
Height	; 26 cm.
Place of publication	– New York
Other title information	: a geographic perspective on natural resource use
Illustration	: ill.
First statement of responsibility	/ by Susan L. Cutter, William H. Renwick
ISBN	ISBN 0-471-01810-4.
Publisher	: Wiley
Edition	. – 3rd ed.
Note	Includes bibliographical references and index.

c.

Date of publication	, 1996
Other title information	: an Inuit legend
ISBN	ISBN 0 48629 117 6.
Pagination	. – 32 p.
Title proper	The owl and the raven
Publisher	: Little Seal Books
Statement of responsibility	/ written down by Lars Svensen
Size	; 26 cm.
Series	– (Tell me a story)
Illustrations	: ill. (some col.)
Place of publication	. – Ottawa

d.

Note	Includes bibliographical references (p. 403-430) and indexes.
Series	– (Oxford studies in social and cultural anthropology)
Illustration	: ill., maps
Statement of responsibility	/ R.H. Barnes
ISBN	ISBN 0 198 28070 X (hardback). – ISBN 0 198 28072 6 (pbk.)
Title proper	Sea hunters of Indonesia
Publisher	: Clarendon Press
Size	; 24 cm.
Place of publication	. – Oxford
Note	Simultaneously published in the USA and Canada.
Other title information	: fishers and weavers of Lamalera
Pagination	. – xvi, 467 p.
Date of publication	, 1996

EXERCISE 2.5

Insert the correct punctuation in the following entries. Use the model on page 28 to identify the punctuation needed to precede each element.

a.

Schaum's outline of theory and problems of intermediate algebra

Ray Steege   New York   McGraw-Hill   c1997   381 p.   ill.   28

cm.

Includes index

ISBN 0-07060-839-3 (pbk.)

b.

Chicken soup for the soul at work   101 stories of courage,

compassion, and creativity in the workplace   Jack Canfield ... [et al.]

Deerfield Beach, Fla.   Health Communications   c1996   xvi, 330 p.

ill.   22 cm.

Includes bibliographical references

ISBN 1-55874-424-X

c.

The discovery of the Titanic   by Robert D. Ballard   with Rick

Archbold   introduction by Walter Lord   illustrations of the Titanic

by Ken Marschall   New York, N.Y.   Warner Books   1987   230 p.

ill. (some col.)   29 cm.

"A Warner/Madison Press Book."

Includes index

ISBN 0-44651-385-7

d.

It's here— somewhere!   Alice Fulton and Pauline Hatch

illustrations by Shunichi Yamamoto   1st ed.   Cincinnati, Ohio

Writer's Digest Books   c1985   179 p.   ill.   23 cm.

Bibliography: p. [174]-175

Includes index

ISBN 0-89879-186-3 (pbk)

EXERCISE 2.6

Identify particular pieces of information in the following descriptions:

a.
Esteticheskaia vyrazitelnost goroda / otvetstvennyi redaktor O. A. Shvidkovskii. – Moskva : Nauka, 1986. – 156 p. : ill. ; 22 cm.
At head of title: Akademiia nauk SSSR.
Includes bibliographical references.

Esteticheskaia vyrazitelnost goroda _____

otvetstvennyi redaktor O. A. Shvidkovskii _____

Moskva _____

Nauka _____

1986 _____

156 p. : ill. ; 22 cm. _____

At head of title: Akademiia nauk SSSR. _____

Includes bibliographical references. _____

b.
Mellan byrakrati och laissez faire : en studie av Camillo Sittes och Patrick Geddes stadsplaneringsstrategier / Lilian Andersson. – Goteborg, Sweden : Acta Universitatis Gothoburgensis, c1989. – 337 p. : ill. ; 25 cm. – (Gothenburg studies in the history of science and ideas ; 9)
Summary in English.
Thesis (doctoral) – Goteborgs universitet, 1989.
Includes bibliographical references (p. 321-334).
ISBN 9 17346 204 7

Mellan byrakrati och laissez faire _____

en studie av Camillo Sittes och Patrick Geddes
stadsplaneringsstrategier _____

Lilian Andersson _____

Goteborg, Sweden _____

Acta Universitatis Gothoburgensis _____

c1989 _____

337 p. : ill. ; 25 cm. _____

(Gothenburg studies in the history of science and ideas ; 9) _____

Summary in English. _____

Thesis (doctoral) — Goteborgs universitet, 1989. _____

Includes bibliographical references (p. 321-334). _____

ISBN 9 17346 204 7. _____

Different Formats of Material

The rules for description of other types of material are also based on the general rules for description—ISBD(G). The differences between the description of monographs and other materials occur when a particular type of material requires more specific information to describe it fully.

Elements of Description

The following outline includes the general names of the elements in the description of all types of material:

Title proper [general material designation] = Parallel title : other title information / first statement of responsibility ; each subsequent statement of responsibility. - Edition statement / first statement of responsibility relating to the edition. - Material (or type of publication) specific details. - First place of publication, etc. : first publisher, etc., date of publication, etc. - Extent of item : other physical details ; dimensions + accompanying material. - (Title proper of series / statement of responsibility relating to series, ISSN of series ; numbering within the series)

Note(s).

Standard number.

EXERCISE 2.7

Here are some records for serials and non-book items. Examine each record and answer the questions about it.

a.   Ground water in pre-Bearpaw Shale Aquifers in the Wolf Point 1x2 quadrangle, northeastern Montana and adjacent North Dakota [map] / by R.N. Bergantino. – Scale 1:250,000 (W 106--W 104 /N 49--N 48). – Butte, Mont. : Montana Bureau of Mines and Geology, 1994. – 1 map : col. ; <u>44 x 59 cm.</u>, on sheet 53 x 73 cm., folded in envelope 30 x 23 cm. – (Montana atlas series ; MA 5-G)
Title from envelope.
Relief shown by contours and spot heights.

What type of material is this? How can you tell?

What is its scale?

What is the underlined element?

b.

Yoga journal's yoga for beginners [videorecording]. – Santa Monica, Calif. : Healing Arts Home Video, c1990. – 1 videocassette (VHS) (75 min) : sd., col. ; 1/2 in. + 1 booklet (51 p. : ill. ; 19 cm.)
<u>Summary: Patricia Walden gives step-by-step instruction in yoga basics: standing poses, seated poses, inverted poses, guidance into breathing awareness and deep relaxation, 3 short-form individual practice sessions.</u>

What type of material is this? How can you tell?

What is the second element of the physical description?

What is the underlined element?

c.

The Journal of human resources. – Vol. 1 (Summer 1966)-   . – Madison : University of Wisconsin Press, 1966-   . – v. ; 24 cm.
Quarterly.
<u>ISSN 0022-166X</u>

What type of material is this? How can you tell?

What does "Vol. 1 (Summer 1966)-   " mean?

What is the underlined element?

d.

Unplugged [music] / Eric Clapton. – Milwaukee, Wis. : Hal Leonard, <u>c1993</u>. – 1 score (72 p.) ; 31 cm.
For voice and piano; with chord symbols and guitar chord diagrams.
Contents: Alberta – Before you accuse me (take a look at yourself) – Hey hey – Layla – Lonely stranger – Malted milk – Nobody knows you when you're down and out – Old love – Rollin' and tumblin' – Running on faith – San Francisco Bay blues – Signe – Tears in heaven – Walkin' blues.

What type of material is this? How can you tell?

What does the note tell you about the kind of music?

What is the underlined element?

e.   Voicing ourselves [electronic resource] : <u>whose words we use when we talk about</u>
<u>books</u> / Christian Knoeller. – Boulder, Colo. : netLibrary, 1999. – Computer data.
Title from title screen.
Includes bibliographical references and index.
Originally published in paper format in 1998 by State University of New York Press.

What type of material is this? How can you tell?

In what other format was this item published? When?

What is the underlined element?

Access Points

In addition to the description of the item, a bibliographic record contains other information. It must include a **heading** or some other indication of the name of the author, title, or other term under which searchers can find the record in the catalog or other listing.

These terms are called **access points** (because they give access to the item). They are selected when the record is created and are determined by the rules used to create the record. The access points may be different for different listings. Listings may have:

- one access point (e.g., a simple bibliography arranged by alphabetical order of author), or
- several access points (e.g., a library catalog, a bibliography with several indexes).

Traditionally, the main access point in a catalog record is called the main entry. This is the access point used when the item is only listed once. It is usually the first-named author or the title. Other names used for access, including titles and organizations, are called added entries. Terms that provide access by describing the content of the item are called subject headings or subject entries.

Catalog cards also include tracing notes, or tracings, that note the other headings under which the work will also be found in the catalog. Since automated systems have evolved from cards or printed records, they follow the same basic rules and formats.

Main entry heading

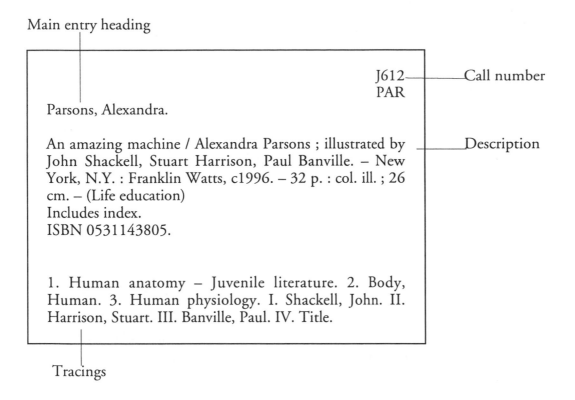

Tracings

Main Entry Heading
When a catalog record is created, the cataloger decides that one of the headings is the main entry heading. This decision is based on the relevant rule(s) in *AACR2*.

Added Entries
Added entries show the other authors, editors, illustrators, translators, titles, series, and organizations by which a client may wish to find the record.

Integrated library systems are becoming increasingly sophisticated in an attempt to make information retrieval easy. Online library catalogs can offer keyword and field searching of the entire bibliographic description, if this is what clients need to find information. Libraries can choose to allow catalog searches for materials using terms such as the publisher, date of publication, ISBN, or even words used in the contents notes.

Subject Headings
The other entries are subject headings given to the work so that a client looking for information on a particular subject can find the work without knowing its author or title.

Classification Numbers

The classification number indicates the subject of the work and sometimes the bibliographic form. There are two major classification schemes:

- Dewey Decimal Classification (DDC)
- Library of Congress Classification (LCC).

There are also several other more specialized classification schemes. Classification is treated in greater detail in Chapter 8.

Dewey Decimal Classification (DDC)

Dewey Decimal Classification uses only numbers to represent the subject. When a DDC number is allocated, a book number is also used. The book number relates to the item itself and usually consists of letters and, occasionally, letters and numbers. It is based on the author or the title of the item. For example:

636.7	classification number
HEW	book number

Library of Congress Classification (LCC)

Library of Congress Classification uses letters and numbers to represent the subject. LCC numbers include the classification number, notation (letters and numbers) that reflects the author or title, and the date of publication. For example:

HQ1593   classification number

.R4
1995   } book number

Location Symbols

The location symbol shows where the item is housed. For example, a reference work may have "R" or "REF"; an audiovisual item may have "AV". Location symbols may also indicate a branch of a library system. They can be used with any classification number.

The combination of notation—including classification, book number, and location symbol—is called the **call number**. For example:

REF	AV
636.7	HQ1593
HEW	.R4
	1995

The call number tells the client exactly where the item is located in the library.

Chapter 3
ASSETS AND ACCESS

Introduction

Libraries acquire materials for the use of their clients in a variety of ways. When a library buys a copy of book, videorecording, and so forth, and stores it, the library is accumulating **assets**. When the library's online catalog points to something on the Internet, for example, and gives clients the opportunity to retrieve information not stored within the library building, the library is providing **access**.

Because most libraries cannot afford to buy all the information sources their clients might want, they combine these two approaches. They buy library materials in the traditional ways as well as obtain access to information stored elsewhere as requested.

This chapter discusses three separate types of work performed in libraries to acquire materials for users:

Acquisitions

Much of acquisitions work involves buying physical materials such as books and videorecordings and storing them in a building for retrieval and use. Electronic books and documents on the Internet are also purchased through acquisitions departments.

Serial Publication Control

Subscriptions to serials, including journals, magazines, and newspapers, usually consume a large percentage of library budgets. The control of serials using manual check-in systems, such as Kardex®, is evolving into the online integrated library system, and the publishing of serials is migrating from print to the online format. Serials are a dynamic and challenging aspect of library services.

Interlibrary Loan

Interlibrary loan allows a library to "lend" items it does not own by borrowing them from other libraries on behalf of a client.

Detailed coverage of issues relating to acquisition and collection development will be available in the forthcoming *Learn acquisitions and collection development* by Jenni Jeremy.

Acquisitions

In a typical acquisitions department, staff purchase or lease (as is frequently the case for electronic products) materials to add to the collection, accept gifts from donors and institutions, and exchange materials with other libraries or information centers. The work of acquisitions includes all or most of the following:

- selecting materials by direct purchase, by donation, or through exchange programs (this is referred to as collection development)
- purchasing items from publishers, distributors, and aggregators (e.g., Proquest, Ebsco); negotiating and corresponding with them
- receiving orders, ensuring that the library receives what it orders and what it pays for
- maintaining accurate in-house records of all transactions
- receiving and processing of donations, issuing tax receipts
- managing exchange agreements with other libraries.

Acquisitions Activities

Basic steps in acquisitions are:

1. Receive requests.
2. Prepare and place orders.
3. Receive items and arrange for payment.
4. Maintain records of all transactions and allocate budgets.
5. Provide liaison between the library and its vendors, suppliers, and publishers.
6. Maintain gifts and exchange agreements and prepare exchange lists.

1. Receive requests

Requests to purchase items might be submitted in print or in electronic format. A library may create a request form for librarians and other staff to complete. It may also accept a photocopy of an advertisement for, or review of, an item, accompanied by an authorized signature and/or budget code. Many web-based catalogs include an online form that registered borrowers can use to send suggestions to the library.

After requests are received, they are put through a pre-order process that involves:

- sorting the requests to detect duplicates and to arrange them in priority order
- confirming that the item is not already on order or in process by consulting the "on order" file or the catalog
- verifying that the item exists and that the bibliographic details, including the price and publisher or supplier, are correct. (Verification work requires problem-solving skills and persistence. See Chapter 5 for more discussion of this topic and for exercises to practice these skills.)

2. Prepare and place orders

Because of the amount of information included in acquisitions records and the fiscal consequences of errors, attention to detail is particularly important when preparing and sending orders.

Records for monograph orders include:

- bibliographic information about the item being ordered (such as title, author, and date of publication)
- price
- number of copies required
- library order number
- library budget code
- supplier's name.

The budget code is the number of the account from which the invoice for the material will be paid. Many libraries divide their budget into several accounts or funds for planning purposes.

In a manual system, the order record is usually a multipart form with the original sent to the supplier and copies kept in an **on-order file**. When the order arrives, the copy of the order is amended to indicate that it has arrived. It is usually removed from the on-order file and placed in a separate **in-process file**. Copies are left in this file until the item is cataloged, when it is transferred to an **orders complete file**.

An example of a manual order form:

Monograph Orders Dept. Coastal Public Library Miami, FL	Order no. 25861 Date 20/04/2000
........1...... copies Markuson, B E and Woods, Blanche (editors) Conference on networks for networkers NY: Neal-Schuman Publishers, 1998 For J Adams	

ISBN	072010159X	CODE	M1012
SUPPLIER	Midwest	PRICE	$62.00

In an automated system, the information is input into the database by staff. Many integrated library systems allow staff to download a record into the database from the Internet and then use it as an order record. The record can be masked from public display or it might be displayed in a brief format showing an on-order status. The system then either prints a purchase form to be sent to the supplier or transmits the record electronically. When the order is received, the relevant fields in the record are updated to reflect its in-process status.

An example of an order record in an automated system:

```
UPDATE ORDER              Status: In process           Verbal Order
─────────────────────────────────────────────────────────────────────
Title           [The acquisition of library material                 ]
Order number    [95000099]
Type            [1  ]                 Date ordered      [17/09/97]
Copies          [    1]               Date requested    [  /  /  ]
Fcc             [    ]                Date received     [  /  /  ]
Price each      [      30.00]         Date paid         [  /  /  ]
Subtotal        [      30.00]         Renewal date      [  /  /  ]
Discount        [          ]          Followup date     [  /  /  ]
Taxes           [          ]          Date cheque req   [  /  /  ]
Misc. charges   [       0.00]         Canceled (Y/N)    [N]
Total order     [      30.00]         Cheque number     [          ]
Vendor acronym  [ALW      ]           Cheque date       [  /  /  ]
Delivery acronym[SOUTH]               Invoice #         [           ]
Action (P/W)    [W]                   Invoice date      [  /  /  ]

Instructions    [                                           ]
─────────────────────────────────────────────────────────────────────
R=Record save          E=Edit            F=Fund accounts      D=Delete
B=Bibliographic                          S=Delivery           ESC=Exit
```

```
UPDATE ORDER              Status: In process           Verbal Order
─────────────────────────────────────────────────────────────────────
Title           [The acquisition of library material                 ]

Type            [1  ]
Author          [Ford, Steven                                        ]
Series          [                                                    ]
Collation       [                                                    ]
Publisher       [Chicago: American Library Association               ]
Volume          [          ]
Issue           [      ]
Year            [1978     ]
ISBN/ISSN       [              ]
Vendor cat#     [          ]
Requester       [                  ]
Edition         [                ]
Call number     [                          ]
Notes           [                                                    ]
─────────────────────────────────────────────────────────────────────
R=Record save                  E=Edit                        ESC=Exit
```

Blanket Orders and Approval Plans

It is not necessary to order everything by individual title. For example, blanket orders and approval plans are alternative methods of acquiring materials. This means that the supplier, using a library's pre-established collection profile, chooses items in particular categories and disciplines. The profile might specify subject area, audience level, format, price range, or language. Blanket orders are usually sent with the understanding that the library will accept everything shipped. Approval plans, however, are subject to inspection and approval and the library can return materials.

3. Receive items and arrange for payment

Receipt of orders includes unpacking boxes, checking documentation, returning errors and defective materials, claiming missing items, and forwarding material for cataloging and processing.

Before unpacking boxes:
- Check the address label and confirm (before signing) that the delivery has been sent to the right address.
- Check for enclosed documentation. This is often found under a plastic label on the outside of the box and is marked "invoice enclosed" or "packing slip enclosed". Note that this means that the documentation is enclosed under the outside label, not inside the box.
- Open the box or boxes carefully. Sharp knives may cut through the contents, not just the packaging.

Occupational Health & Safety Alert
Boxes of books are heavy. Move them carefully and ensure that the weight is evenly distributed on book trucks or they may topple over.

Unpack the box and sort the books alphabetically, especially if you have a large number of items arriving at one time. This makes checking against the invoice much easier.

Check inside the box for:
- invoices
- packing slips
- statements
- order reports
- publishers' brochures.

After checking the address, unpacking the boxes, and locating the documentation:

- **Check the items received against the invoice or packing slip.**
  Ensure that the items match those included on the documentation and that all items on the invoice or packing slip are actually included.

- **Check for damage as you unpack or as you check against the invoice.**
  Physical damage should be referred to a supervisor. In some cases, the decision may be made to accept the item if the damage is minimal or if the item has proved difficult to acquire.

- **Check the item received against the on-order record.**
  Verify that you have the item your library ordered. Pay particular attention to:
    - ISBN
    - author/title
    - edition
    - dates of publication
    - number of copies
    - format (paperback, hardcover, large print, AV).

  Not all differences mean that the item received is unacceptable. A different edition from the one ordered, such as a later edition of a popular work or a differently bound edition, may be acceptable. In these cases, the order record will have to be amended to reflect the actual item received.

- **Check the price.**
  Check the invoiced price against the price quoted on the library purchase order. Usually, the negotiated terms of trade between a supplier and a library, or the library's original order to the supplier, will state an acceptable price variation. If the price variation is greater than agreed upon, the supplier should have notified the library before sending the item, giving the library the opportunity to cancel or confirm the order. If the supplier breaches this condition, the library is justified in returning the item. Invoices may also need to be checked to ensure that other entitlements such as discounts have been received. In a manual system, the order record should be amended to indicate the actual price paid. This information is useful if additional copies are ordered at a later stage.

- **Arrange payment of invoice.**
  In large institutions, this might involve sending the necessary documentation authorizing payment to an Accounts Payable department. In small operations, you might mail a check or authorize an account debit. Once money in an account or fund has been aside to pay for items the library has received, the amount is said to be **encumbered**.

  In automated acquisitions systems, the order record is updated by adding a received date or by changing the status from "On order" to "Received". Then the invoice (the document that requests payment from the library) is processed. The invoice lists the items supplied and their cost. The library's order number for each individual item should be quoted on the invoice.

  The invoice may also include information about the terms of payment. The total cost invoiced may differ from the sum of the individual items if there are additional line items such as discounts or freight charges.

  Invoices may be sent separately from the materials themselves, especially in the case of overseas items. They are usually sent airmail in advance of the parcel. This allows the library to know what is due and makes it easier to follow up on items that are not received.

  Invoices may also be sent electronically.

An example of an invoice:

	BEST LIBRARY SERVICES 20 CROSS ST., CHICAGO			
		INVOICE NO: 1- 956 DATE: 5/5/00		
TO COASTAL PUBLIC LIBRARY Miami, FL				
ORDER NO	AUTHOR /TITLE	COPIES	UNIT COST	TOTAL COST
25846	Markuson, B E and Woods, Blanche Conference on networks for networkers	1	61.50	35.00
25741	Beyond 1984: the future of library technical services	1	42.56	50.72
24973	Anglo-American cataloguing rules: Chapter 6 Chicago: American Library Association, 1974	1	27.60	27.60
26017	Olle, James Library history	1	26.50	26.50
25948	Becker, J and Pulsifer, J S Application of computer technology to libraries	1	17.30	17.30
25689	Sherman, S ABCs of library promotion 2nd ed.	2	20.20	40.40
25932	Dobson, James Preparing for adolescence	1	32.60	32.60
	SUBTOTAL			230.12
	Freight			22.50
	TOTAL			252.62

4. Maintain records of all transactions and allocate budgets

Libraries are accountable for the funds they receive. Therefore, staff should keep accurate records of all transactions to document how the money is spent.

Acquisitions staff may also assist with the preparation of budget statements and with the allocation of the acquisitions budget among the various funds or accounts. For these reasons, bookkeeping and accounting skills are important in this type of work.

5. Provide liaison between the library and its vendors, suppliers, and publishers

Acquisitions staff provide the link between the library and the various agencies with which it does business. Libraries might purchase items from trade publishers who sell materials that appeal to a wide general audience. Often, however, they prefer to deal with wholesalers who handle trade books from various publishers to save the time of negotiating and corresponding with many individual publishers. Academic and special libraries may need to buy materials directly from publishers who produce books in specific fields or disciplines. Medical, legal, and scientific and technical publishers, university presses, private presses, and government departments supply items that trade publishers do not carry because the market for this information is small and sales are limited.

Electronic Publishing

Also called "publishing on demand", electronic publishing includes online serials, books, videorecordings, and music. Information transferred in digital form over local networks and the Internet saves the publisher the expense of printing and storing materials. Electronic publishing puts a heavy burden on the user to obtain access to a computer and printer in order to access and use the information.

6. Maintain gifts and exchange agreements and prepare exchange lists

Many libraries accept donations of books and other materials to add to the collections. Most donations are unsolicited and are offered to a library when someone moves or empties out their office. Donated materials often need to be evaluated because donors frequently expect a tax receipt.

Libraries set up arrangements to exchange materials with each other. Usually, a group of libraries will agree to produce and exchange lists of unwanted and duplicate materials (such as issues of serials) on a regular basis. The first library to request an item on the list gets the item and pays to have it shipped.

Gifts and exchanges save the cost of purchasing the information but still require an investment of staff time to receive the items, to determine if they are suitable for the collection, and then to catalog and process them for circulation to library users. These materials may be recorded in the acquisitions files in the same way as ordered items but without the financial information. "Gift" or "exchange" may replace the supplier information.

EXERCISE 3.1

1.   Visit Acqweb on the Internet at http://acqweb.library.vanderbilt.edu/

    a) What are the current hot topics of interest to acquisitions staff?

    b) Find an online currency converter.

    c) What are approval plans? Find a description of one on a library vendor's website.

2.   Under what circumstances might a library keep an item that wasn't exactly what was ordered?

Serial Publication Control

The term **serial** refers to a publication issued in separate parts. The parts, or issues, are numbered (e.g., vol. 10, no. 3) or have chronological designations (e.g., January 2001). A serial is intended to be published indefinitely, meaning there is no end date of publication in mind when the first issue is published. They are generally issued regularly (monthly, bimonthly, etc.), although this is not mandatory. Serials may be in any medium: print, microform, electronic, videorecording, and so forth.

Careful control of incoming issues of serials enables a library to get maximum value for its subscription dues. Serial control systems vary, but most can answer the following questions:

- What is the latest issue received?
- Are any issues missing or unavailable for some other reason?
- How often does the library send issues for binding?
- Where can one subscribe to the publication?
- When is the library's subscription due for renewal?

Because serials are published over a period of time, they often undergo many changes. A serial might:

- cease publication permanently or temporarily
- change titles
- merge with another title to become a new serial
- change size or format
- split into two separate titles
- publish special issues or supplements, sometimes with separate titles
- change publishers or subject matter.

Many serials are also published electronically and made available on the Internet. They are called e-journals and are often packaged together by publisher or subject and sold to libraries by **aggregators.**

Aggregators are agencies that acquire the distribution rights for different pieces of information and then offer the pieces as a package. Aggregators sell libraries web-based full-text databases that include journals, magazines, and newspapers in electronic format. These journals, magazines, and newspapers are often all published separately. The aggregator negotiates licenses with the publishers and then distributes the information with "added value" services such as a search engine and the option to send documents to an email address.

Electronic serials are often more complex to manage because they are not shipped to the library as are print materials, but are accessed over networks. User names, passwords, and Internet addresses are features of electronic serials subscriptions that the print versions do not require.

Acquisitions staff may assist with the setting up of test accounts for an electronic package to be evaluated by librarians and library users such as faculty. They might also coordinate the signing of license agreements and communicate with systems staff regarding passwords and links from the online catalog.

Control of Print Serial Titles

This chapter focuses on receiving print subscriptions and maintaining their check-in records. The procedure for receiving serial issues is the same for manual and automated systems. **Check-in record** refers to either a manual or an automated file. The serials control steps include:

1. Check the address label to ensure that issues have arrived at the correct destination.
2. Open and inspect for damage; check for accompanying information; retain packaging.
3. Sort into priority order.
4. Locate the check-in record.
5. Record receipt carefully and accurately.
6. Stamp the issue and process by adding call numbers, barcodes, and so on, according to library policy.
7. Notify cataloging staff if any information has changed (e.g., title change, ceased publication, new supplement included).
8. Attach routing slips for circulated titles.
9. Claim late issues.

1. Check the address label to ensure that issues have arrived at the correct destination

2. Open and inspect for damage; check for accompanying information; retain packaging

Items in poor condition and not suitable for client use should be replaced. However, a substitute copy may not always be available and is usually requested only in cases where there is substantial damage.

Accompanying material may be:

- renewal invoices
- notices of change of title
- notice of ceasing or suspended publication
- advertising material
- notices of conferences.

Renewal notices should be routed to the appropriate person for processing. Change of title and/or publication information requires amendment of the check-in record. Advertising material is given to selection staff. Notices of conferences may be kept with the issue, displayed separately, or sent to clients according to their interests.

The packaging should be kept with the issue in case it includes details the person updating the check-in record will need. The packaging may also provide reference numbers that can be used to trace orders.

3. Sort into priority order

If many titles are being received, the serials may be sorted alphabetically by title, by date of receipt, or in priority order for processing. Titles received by airmail, as well as daily and weekly publications, are usually processed as a priority.

4. Locate the check-in record

Locate the record for the title in hand by searching the library's file of check-in records. Manual files are usually kept on cards and arranged by title. Automated files are generally searched by title, ISSN, or SICI (Serial Item and Contribution Identifier)—a barcode attached by the publisher to make serials check-in more efficient. Libraries with automated serials systems can scan the SICI barcode and the system then records the issue as received.

Check carefully that the title in hand matches the serial check-in record. Libraries may receive several serials with similar titles or there may be a title change or merger.

Verify that the expected issue has arrived, whether an issue has been missed, or whether the one in hand is actually a duplicate copy. Look for the issue information on front cover, the title page, or the spine. The information may be:
- a chronological designation (e.g., 5/5/98 or 5 May 1998 or Fall 1998)
- a volume and number designation (e.g., Vol. 16, no. 4)
- a number (e.g., No. 1345)
- a combination of the above.

5. Record receipt carefully and accurately

In both automated and manual systems, attention to detail is essential, and the work often calls for some problem solving. It is important to record the exact issues and date of receipt. Consistent and accurate data entry provides staff and library users with comprehensive holdings information and saves the time and effort often spent looking for "missing" issues.

Manual System

In a manual system, the title information is recorded in a grid. Each box of the grid shows the date or number of the issue. The date of receipt is entered into the grid box to record receipt. A blank box means that the issue has not yet been received.

It is recommended that staff involved in serials check-in:
- Use the pattern of previous receipts as a guide when entering a new receipt.
- Leave a space for a missing issue if the issue currently being received is later than the one due to be received.
- Remember that it is important in a manual system to be very neat recording information in the small spaces provided.

Example of a manual check-in card:

Supplier				Frequency			Call Number					
Faxon				Quarterly			QB351 .Q2					

Price				Order no			No of copies					
$725.60				9458			1					

Subscription Paid				Period held			Binding					
01/10/2000				2000 –			Annual					

Holdings Policy

KEEP INDEFINITELY   DISPLAY

Year	Vol	Jan	Feb	Mar	Apr	May	Jun	Jul	Aug	Sep	Oct	Nov	Dec
2000	24												
2001	25												
2002	26												
2003	27												

Title Quarterly Review of Studies in Celestial Mechanics

Notes   Route to BM, LB, TR

Automated System

In an automated system, the issue is recorded in a grid or a list. Most online serial control systems can be set to enter the current date as the date of receipt and display the next expected issue. You can accept this or edit the issue date if it is different from the expected issue.

The checking, routing, and binding records are usually a series of linked screens.

Example of a serial record in an automated system:

```
SERIAL UPDATE                                        Journal/Toc: 6/0

 Acronym       [CHA      ]
 Title         [Challenge                                         ]
 Call number   [330 CHA                    ]
 Location      [main                   ]

 ISSN          [            ] Type          [   ]
 Vendor        [ALW     ]     Invoice #     [              ]
 Title #       [          ]   Account #     [               ]

 Order date    [17/03/98]     Current cost  [     40.00]
 Renew date    [ /  /  ]      Last cost     [      0.00]
 Date canceled [ /  /  ]

 Frequency     [BM]           Issue due     [JUL-AUG 1998        ]
 Checkin type  [10]           Due date      [15/11/98]

 R=Record save    S=Subject      J=Journal slip   B=Bindings
 E=Edit           H=Holdings     T=TOC slip       G=Grace/Notes
```

SUBSCRIPTION HISTORY					
Issue	Status	Check-in date	Status date	Due	Next Action
MAY-JUNE, 1998	REC	16/09/98	16/09/98	15/09/98	
MAR-APR, 1998	REC	15/07/98	15/07/98	15/07/98	
JAN-FEB, 1998	CLAIM2		25/08/98	15/05/98	25/09/98
NOV-DEC, 1997	REC	12/03/98	12/03/98	15/03/98	

Note: Display Keep 2 years   Call No: 330 CHA
Location: Main library   Frequency: Bi-monthly

R = Record save   E = Edit   P = Print
I = Insert   D = Delete

Automated serial records keep track of:

- which titles are currently being received
- which issues of inactive titles are held (sometimes in a separate file)
- which titles are on order or in process
- when issues of each title are received and an estimate of when the next issue is due
- processing information such as location, call number, holdings policy, binding information
- special instructions for cataloging serial issues individually
- supply problems such as missing issues, lapsed subscriptions, and the action taken
- order and renewal information (e.g., supplier, order number)
- a history of payments.

Many online systems can be set up to print routing slips and claim forms.

6. Stamp the issue and process

- Stamp the issue with the library's ownership stamp, which often includes the date received.
- Mark the issue with the call number, taking care that labels do not cover important information, such as the title, volume number, or date.
- Attach barcodes, date due labels, security strips, and so on, according to library policy.

7. Notify cataloging staff if any information has changed

If it appears that a title has changed, has ceased publication, or has arrived with a new supplement, route to the cataloging department. Catalog records for serials can be updated to include notes explaining variant titles, accompanying supplements, and publishing information.

8. Attach routing slips for circulated titles

Journal circulation or routing means sending new serial issues to selected library clients. Serials staff might circulate a list of all the titles the library is willing to circulate and ask users to indicate what they wish to see. This service is often offered by special libraries to their users and by academic or school libraries to staff. Such a service is good public relations.

Journal circulation puts the information in people's hands and allows them to read it when it arrives, without having to monitor the library's new issues shelves. Clients like the service and it makes them aware of the library.

When an issue arrives and is checked in, a prepared list of clients is attached to the issue that is then routed to the first person on the list. Occasionally you may need to add or remove names from the list.

The downside of routing is that it may be impossible to know exactly where an issue is or when it will return. The library is therefore required to encourage people to read and pass on the issues in a timely manner to the next person on the routing list.

9. Claim late issues

Serials are complex, and their ongoing maintenance and control is labor-intensive. For this reason, many libraries employ subscription agents to help them manage serial subscriptions. If the library does not have a subscription agent, claims are sent directly to the publisher or distributor.

Late issues are common, and serials are known to be unpredictable. After a number of weeks or months, the library might send a claim notice to inquire about the status of a title (e.g., Has it ceased or been suspended?) The claim notice might be a form letter, either typed by hand or generated from the online system. Keep in mind that claiming too quickly after the expected date might result in duplicate issues.

Some received and circulated issues might not be in any condition to go for binding when the time comes. It is sometimes necessary to re-order missing and damaged issues from either the subscription agent or the publisher, often at a higher price.

EXERCISE 3.2

Lists of catalogs available on the Internet include:
Acqweb http://acqweb.library.vanderbilt.edu/acqweb/verif_cats.html
LibDex http://www.libdex.com/

1. Compare the display of serial records in four different library catalogs on the Internet for three or four serial titles. Does the OPAC record display information about the latest issue received and tell you where to find it? What other information is included?

2. What are some of the differences between the control of print and electronic journal subscriptions?

Interlibrary Loan

Interlibrary loan (ILL) is the process of borrowing material from another library on behalf of a client. When a library does not own a book or other piece of information that a borrower requests, ILL is an efficient way to meet the information need. Library staff search for the item in other library catalogs to locate a library system that owns the item and is willing to lend it.

ILL is a reciprocal relationship, and libraries should be willing to lend materials if they want to borrow.

National Interlibrary Loan Code for the United States

The full text of the code is available on the American Library Association's website: http://www.ala.org/rusa/stnd_lnc.html

The code is also available in print in the Summer 1994 issue of *RQ* (v. 33 no. 4, pp. 477- 479).

The code is intended to regulate lending and borrowing relations among libraries in the United States and to encourage the exchange of material.

Interlibrary Loan in Canada

The ILL directory on the Web, available at http://www.nlc-bnc.ca/ill/e-ill.htm, provides a searchable interface to the publication *Symbols and interlibrary loan policies in Canada*. The directory lists libraries participating in ILL and provides their mailing addresses, telephone and fax numbers, electronic mail addresses, and policy information.

National guidelines for document delivery, available online at the above web address, provides guidelines for document delivery in Canada and recommends various methods of sending requests and delivering documents.

Libraries should avoid:

- requesting reference materials and materials in high demand
- sending all requests to the same one or two libraries
- borrowing and lending materials that do not comply with copyright laws.

Libraries should borrow locally first and work primarily with libraries that borrow from them.

Lending Procedures

1. Receive and prioritize requests.
2. Decide if the library should accept the request by considering the consortium, state, or regional codes that apply, as well as the copyright laws.
3. Locate the item in the collection.
4. Copy/lend/send a report on why it is not being loaned.
5. Record payment or debit the other library's account.
6. Package and send the item.
7. Receive items returned from ILL.

1. Receive and prioritize requests

ILL requests arrive in a number of ways:

- by mail
- by telephone (not recommended)
- by fax
- by email
- electronically via ILL networks such as RLIN or OCLC.

ILL networks that allow electronic transmission are busy and require the commitment of staff and equipment. Faxed ALA-approved interlibrary loan forms are quick but can incur long-distance bills. The following interlibrary loan form is available for downloading at http://www.ala.org/rusa/stnd_illformprint.html

Interlibrary Loan Request Form

Request No.: Date: Need before: Notes:

Call No.:

(Borrowing Address Here)

Patron information:
Book author, OR, Serial title, volume, issue, date, pages; OR Audiovisual title:

Book title, edition, imprint series; OR, Article author, title:
    This edition only

Verified in; AND/OR Cited in:

ISBN, ISSN, LCCN, or other bibliographic number:

(Lending Address Here)

Request complies with   Authorization: _____
[ ] 108(g) (2) Guidelines (CCG)

[ ] other provision of copyright law (CCL)

     Telephone: _____

TYPE OF REQUEST:

[ ]   LOAN; WILL PAY FEE _____

[ ]   PHOTOCOPY; MAX COSTS ___

[ ]

LENDING LIBRARY REPORT: Date

Date shipped:_____ via _____

Insured for $ _____Charge $ _____

DUE _____ [ ] Return insured

Packing Requirements

RESTRICTIONS: [ ] Library use only

[ ] Copying not permitted

[ ] No renewals [ ] _____

NOT SENT BECAUSE:

[ ] In use [ ] Lacking [ ] Not owned

[ ] At bindery [ ] Cost exceeds limit

[ ] Non Circulating [ ] Lost

[ ] Not found as cited [ ] On order

[ ] Not found on shelf

[ ] Lacks copyright compliance

[ ] In process [ ] Request on _____

[ ] Hold placed [ ] Poor Condition

[ ] Estimate Cost of Loan $ _____

Photocopy $ _____ Microfilm/fiche $ ____

[ ] Prepayment required

BORROWING LIBRARY REPORT:

Date received _____ Date returned _____

Returned via _____ Insured for $ ____

Payment provided $ _____

RENEWALS:

Date requested _____

New due date _____

Renewal denied _____

Determine the priority order of the requests based on your library's policy. For example, consortium agreements might specify that members' requests receive priority over other libraries. Watch for requests that are marked "Rush" or have "Not wanted after" dates.

2. Should the library accept the request?

In accepting the request, your library needs to decide:

- Does it conform to the ILL code?
- Does it breach copyright law?

You may reject requests for high-use material, valuable or fragile material, or reference material. Libraries may also refuse to lend to a distant library if the item can be borrowed from a much closer library.

It is the requesting library's responsibility to ensure that requests for copies of items conform to copyright law and to keep all the necessary records. The supplying library, however, should not provide copies that are obviously in breach of the law.

Libraries are permitted to copy material for another library if:

- the copy will not be used for commercial or business purposes. For example, copyright materials can be reproduced for use in the classroom.
- the library collections are open to the public or the library collections are meant to serve the needs of students and researchers
- the copy includes a notice of copyright.

3. Locate the item

Requests might arrive with call numbers included if the requesting libraries have looked them up in your online catalog. When the call number is supplied with the request, some libraries still check all requests first in the catalog; others check the shelves first. It might save time to confirm that the item is available before going to the stacks to retrieve it. Items might be on loan, out being repaired, missing, or in special collections. If a requested item is on loan and due to be returned in time to meet the request, put a hold on it.

The requesting library should be informed promptly if the request will be delayed or not supplied. The requesting library should include a "date not required after" with the original request. If you cannot supply by that date, notify the requesting library immediately. If no date is given, assume the material will be required indefinitely.

4. Copy/lend/send a report on why it is not being loaned

Copying

Photocopies of articles from journals and chapters from books are usually sent with the understanding that they will not be returned. This service is called **document delivery** and may be subject to a per item fee.

Copying library materials should be done with care:
- Do not damage items by forcing spines flat.
- Copy carefully so that the copy is readable and the edges of paragraphs are visible.
- Include all pages.
- Use sufficient exposure to ensure legibility.

Copyright
Libraries that participate in ILL activities must display copyright warnings prominently and comply with the copyright law when lending to and borrowing from other libraries. They are required to maintain transaction records for a rolling three years in addition to the current year.

Lending Materials
Items being loaned should be checked out through the circulation system so that local staff and clients know they are not available. Loan periods for ILL should take transit time as well as patron use time into account.

Reports on Nonfulfillment
If for any reason you are unable to fulfill a request, reply promptly so the requesting library knows to ask elsewhere.

Request Format	Notification Action
Mail requests (form)	Fill in the reports section of the form and return by mail.
Mail requests (letter)	Add a message to a copy of the request and return by mail.
Fax	Add a message to a copy of the request and return by fax.
Email	Use the reply command to add a short reply to the message received and return by email.
Electronically via an ILL network	Fill in the appropriate field to explain the reason the loan was refused. The reply is sent via the system.

5. Record payment
Most large libraries with well-stocked collections charge other libraries a lending fee to offset the staff and resource costs of providing ILL. Smaller libraries might form partnerships to lend and borrow among a group without charging fees.

If your library charges other libraries a lending fee, you might send a monthly invoice or debit a deposit account. ILL networks use online systems to send and receive requests and to keep track of transactions and process payments.

6. Package and send the item
Material for loan may be sent via an overnight courier, registered mail, or some other reasonably secure carrier.

Loans are put in wrappers identifying the lending library and the conditions of loan, such as for in-library use only. Many libraries include a return address sticker to ensure the item is returned to the correct address. Padded bags are used to prevent damage.

Photocopies are sent via the standard mail service or faxed. They usually include a compliments slip and may have an invoice attached.

A copy of the request should be sent with the loan for easy identification.

7. Receive returned items

Upon return, items must be discharged in the circulation system and reshelved. The lending library might receive a credit note or have funds transferred into an account, as payment for loans. ILL records should be updated and moved to a completed file. Libraries might use the completed file to compile annual statistics, monitor the costs of participating in ILL, and report income generated by fees and late fines.

Borrowing Procedures

Here are the standard steps for borrowing items:

1. Advertise the service.
2. Verify bibliographic details and sources.
3. Prepare and transmit borrowing request.
4. Receive materials and notify client.
5. Return materials to lending library.

1. Advertise the service

Signs and flyers can be used to inform clients of the service and of any applicable fees. Make ILL request forms available for users to fill out, noting the required bibliographic information. Forms for book and journal article requests can be printed on different colors of paper to make it easier for staff to sort them. Online catalogs accessed over the Internet often allow clients to submit forms electronically, using information retrieved during an OPAC search.

Whether to charge clients a fee for ILL service is a matter of policy. Some libraries might subsidize the cost of borrowing for their users. Other may have to pass the costs along to users in order to continue to provide ILL service.

2. Verify bibliographic details and sources

Before asking another library to lend you something, you must confirm that the item exists and that the bibliographic information is accurate. You can do this by finding it in an online database, authoritative bibliography, or index. Large online library catalogs are very useful for this, especially union catalogs that merge more than one library's holdings into one database (e.g., OCLC and RLIN).

3. Prepare and transmit borrowing request

The telephone is not ideal for interlibrary loan because it interrupts the work of the receiving library. Information can be copied incorrectly, wasting staff time. Unless a previous agreement has been made, the telephone is usually not acceptable—even for very urgent requests.

Faxing is quick and provides both parties with an exact copy of the request.

4. Receive materials and notify client
Confirm that the received materials match your record of the request. Loans often arrive with an ILL transaction number from the lender or return address shipping labels. Keep these with your records.

Notify your client that the material has arrived and where it can be retrieved—usually the circulation desk or ILL office. Libraries might route the item to the client by courier or interdepartmental mail. Include a clear indication of the due date with the item, taking into account the time it will take to mail or courier it back to the lending library.

5. Return materials to lending library
Materials returned past the due date will likely incur fines as well as inconvenience the lending library. Materials should be sent back on time and in the same condition in which they were received.

Revision Quiz 3.3

1. Name four ways (other than by telephone) in which libraries receive ILL requests from other libraries.

2. Name three types of material that libraries prefer not to lend.

3. What methods do libraries use to send items loaned through ILL?

4. Under what circumstances are libraries permitted to copy material for another library?

5. Public and academic library websites often include ILL information for clients and for other libraries. Search the Internet to find a library's procedure manual for interlibrary loan or a description of the lending policies.

Chapter 4
THE CATALOG

Catalog Records

The card catalog, the book catalog, and the microfiche catalog were the most common formats of library catalogs when catalog records were manually produced. The online catalog, usually referred to as the OPAC (online public access catalog), is currently the preferred format because it uses computer technology to search and retrieve information. Regardless of the catalog format, catalog records are created using the same cataloging tools and contain the same essential bibliographic information. The most important difference is the number of ways in which information can be retrieved.

Traditionally, catalogers determined the access points in the catalog by, for example, typing up a set of cards and filing them by author, title, and subject. In online catalogs, however, it is possible to have many more access points. In theory, every element in a record is searchable, depending on the system software. For example, a user can search for a book by the ISBN if the OPAC software allows this type of search.

EXERCISE 4.1

Highlight all the access points you might expect in this online catalog record.

CALL NO	574.9992 H816
AUTHOR	Horowitz, Norman Harold, 1915-
TITLE	To utopia and back : the search for life in the solar system / Norman H. Horowitz.
PUBLISHER	New York : W. H. Freeman, c1986.
DESCRIPT'N	xiii, 168 p., [8] p. of plates : ill. (some col.) ; 24 cm.
ISBN	1) 0716717662 (pbk.)
	2) 0716717654 (hard)
NOTE(S)	1) Includes index.
	2) Bibliography: p. [151]-159.
SUBJECT	1) Viking Mars Program (U.S.)
	2) Life on other planets.
	3) Mars (Planet) -- Exploration.

Authority Control

Authority control is the maintenance of standard forms of headings found in the catalog. This enables library users to locate information using consistent subject and name headings.

Catalogers record decisions about the standard forms of headings, as well as the research that they have done to make those decisions, in an authority file. This file can be shared by the staff of one cataloging department or even by a consortium of libraries so that other catalogers do not have to re-create headings or research them again. References made to and from the headings are also recorded in this file.

References

A reference is a direction or signpost in the catalog from one heading to another so that library users can find all related entries.

Once catalogers have established a heading for an author or a subject, they create references in the catalog to refer users from other headings that they might search. By doing this, the catalog provides directions from headings that are not used to the headings that are in use. Directions to and from related headings are also made.

Authority Records

There are four types of authority records: name, subject, series, and uniform title. Name authority files generally include uniform titles and series in addition to personal and corporate names.

Establishing name authority records involves the use of part two of *AACR2* to determine the correct form of the heading. Catalogers might also use reference sources such as *Who's who in America* or the *American national biography* to find dates of birth or the full form of names.

Most North American libraries establish their subject headings using *Library of Congress subject headings*. Many school libraries use the *Sears list of subject headings*, published by H. W. Wilson.

Authority Files

Libraries might maintain a local authority file, or use authority files available online or on microfiche, to find and verify headings for their catalog.

The largest authority file for names is the *Library of Congress name authorities*. Libraries can purchase access to the online version from vendors, such as Marcive and AutoGraphics, or buy a subscription to the Cumulative Microform Edition from the Cataloging Distribution Service, Library of Congress.

The major authority file for subjects is the *Library of Congress subject headings*. This file is available by subscription in print as a multivolume set (issued annually), on microfiche (updated quarterly), and on CD-ROM as part of the *Cataloger's desktop* (also updated quarterly) from the Library of Congress.

Large cataloging networks, such as OCLC and RLIN, also maintain their own authority files. These files are a valuable resource because they contain entries created by member libraries that are not included in the Library of Congress files.

Types of References

See Reference

A *see* reference directs the user from a heading that is not used to a heading that is used. *See* references are useful when:

- An author uses a pseudonym for all or some published works.
- An author changes name.
- A different form of name appears on different works by the same person (e.g., Jean A. Smith, Jean Audrey Smith, J. A. Smith).
- There is confusion about which part of a name to use; for example, a searcher may not know whether to look for the French writer Jean de la Fontaine under "de", "la" or "Fontaine".

These signposts are displayed in online public access catalogs in a variety of ways. Here is an example:

```
19.   Franklin, Stella Maria Sarah Miles, 1879-1954
20.         See:  Franklin, Miles, 1879-1954
```

In this example, the author used "Miles Franklin" rather than her full name on her works. The library chose to enter records for all of her works under this form of her name.

If the searcher selects "20" for the heading established in the authority file under which all items by this author are found in the collection, the catalog will provide a list of the these items.

If the searcher chooses "19" to select Franklin, Stella Maria Sarah Miles, 1879-1954, the catalog offers this help:

```
Franklin, Stella Maria Sarah Miles, 1879-1954  is not used in this library's catalog;
Franklin, Miles, 1879-1954 is used instead.
Do you wish to  search for Franklin, Miles, 1879-1954?  (y/n)
```

See Also Reference

A *see also* reference directs the catalog user to a related entry or name. It is normally used when a person or corporate body is entered under two or more different names. This happens most often when corporate bodies change their names. For example:

```
League of Nations Library.
     see also
          United Nations Library (Geneva, Switzerland)
```

Explanatory Reference

An explanatory reference provides more detailed guidance than is given in a *see* or *see also* reference. For example:

League of Red Cross and Red Crescent Societies.
> (In 1983 the League of Red Cross Societies changed its name to League of Red Cross and Red Crescent Societies. In November 1991 the League of Red Cross and Red Crescent Societies changed its name to International Federation of Red Cross and Red Crescent Societies.)
> see also former name
>> League of Red Cross Societies
> see also later name
>> International Federation of Red Cross and Red Crescent Societies

Explanatory references are included in major authority files to share cataloging decisions. They are also used in the authority files of individual libraries to explain particular cataloging usage and practices.

Authority Records

Here are some examples of authority records:

Funny bone
> UF   Crazy bone
>> Funnybone
> BT   Elbow

This record gives **Funny bone** as the correct form of the heading. Each of the *UF* (used for) references gives a nonpreferred form of the heading. An OPAC search for **Crazy bone** would result in a *see* reference to the term Funnybone. The *BT* (broader term) reference provides users with a broader term for use if appropriate.

Cheyney University
> UF   Cheyney University of Pennsylvania
>> Pennsylvania. Cheyney University

> Named Cheyney University of Pennsylvania since 1983; est. in 1837 as an agricultural school under Quaker control; chartered as Institute for Colored Youth in 1842; was Cheyney State College in 1959.

> See also former name
>> Cheyney State College

This *explanatory* reference indicates that the name of this organization changed. The name of the organization in use at the time of publication is the form of the name added to a catalog record for an item by or about the organization.

```
Nossal, Gustav, Sir, 1931-
      SEE Nossal, G. J. V. (Gustav Joseph Victor), Sir, 1931-

Nossal, Gustav Joseph Victor, Sir, 1931-
      SEE Nossal, G. J. V. (Gustav Joseph Victor), Sir, 1931-
```

This OPAC display gives **Nossal, G. J. V. (Gustav Joseph Victor), Sir, 1931-** as the correct form of the heading. The other forms of the heading are nonpreferred headings, and the catalog displays *see* references for each of them.

```
Armstrong, Louis, 1900-1971
      x      Armstrong, Satchmo, 1900-1971
      x      Satchmo, 1900-1971
      x      Louis Armstrong

Armstrong, Satchmo, 1900-1971
      See   Armstrong, Louis, 1900-1971

Satchmo, 1900-1971
      See   Armstrong, Louis, 1900-1971

Louis Armstrong
      See   Armstrong, Louis, 1900-1971
```

This display gives **Armstrong, Louis, 1900-1971** as the correct form of the heading. Each of the *x* references gives a non-preferred form of the heading, which a library user might use as a search term.

EXERCISE 4.2

Look carefully at the catalog displays below, and answer the following questions.

a.   6. Pound, Nathan Roscoe, 1870-1964
       7. See: Pound, Roscoe, 1870-1964.

i.   Which is the preferred heading?

ii.   Does this library use the heading "Pound, Nathan Roscoe, 1870-1964" for any works by this author?

b.

Society for Horticultural Science (U.S.)
See also American Society for Horticultural Science

i.   Is the heading "Society for Horticultural Science (U.S.)" used in this catalog?

ii.   Is the heading " American Society for Horticultural Science" used?

EXERCISE 4.3

Look carefully at the display below, and answer the following questions.

a.   1. Plaidy, Jean, 1906-
       2. See also Carr, Philippa, 1906-
       3. See also Ford, Elbur, 1906-
       4. See also Holt, Victoria, 1906-
       5. See also Kellow, Kathleen, 1906-

i.   Which is the heading to be used for this person in the catalog?

ii.   What will happen if a client searches for "Holt, Victoria"?

iii.   Do all entries refer to the same person?

b.   United States. Immigration and Naturalization Service

The name of the United States Bureau of Immigration (established on July 12, 1891) was
changed to Bureau of Immigration and Naturalization on June 29, 1906. On March 14, 1913, the
Bureau was divided to form the Bureau of Naturalization and the Bureau of Immigration
(thereby resuming a former name). On June 10, 1933, the two bureaus merged to form the
Immigration and Naturalization Service.

RT   United States. Bureau of Immigration
       United States. Bureau of Naturalization

    i.   Which is the heading to be used for this organization in the catalog?

    ii.   What does RT stand for?

    iii.   Might a catalog contain all three headings? Under what circumstances?

MARC

MARC stands for MAchine Readable Cataloging. The MARC format is an international standard. It is a "carrier" of bibliographic information, in a form that computers can read and manipulate. MARC was developed to allow libraries to share cataloging by providing a format that can be read and understood by different library information systems. Today there are millions of MARC records available, with more created daily by catalogers all over the world.

MARC **bibliographic** records consist of bibliographic descriptions of library materials, including books, serials, videorecordings, maps, and electronic resources.

MARC **authority** records consist of established headings, *see* references, and, sometimes, notes that indicate the scope of a heading and the tools consulted to establish the heading.

MARC 21 is the current edition of the standard. It is a harmonization of USMARC and CANMARC, which were slightly different. Australian libraries also use MARC 21. Most British libraries use UKMARC; UNIMARC is used by some European libraries. Other MARC formats are similar to MARC 21, but there are some differences.

Fields

In all databases, a record is a collection of related fields. The fields in a record in a MARC database contain the bibliographic information that forms the bibliographic record. These include the eight areas of description, the access points, the subject headings and the classification numbers.

The MARC record also contains fields that provide information required by the computer. These fields will not be discussed here. (For more details of the MARC record, see Chapter 5 of Mary Mortimer's *Learn descriptive cataloging*.)

Tags

Each field has an identifying label. This label is called a tag and is comprised of three characters. For example, tag 245 identifies the title and statement of responsibility field.

Indicators

Two additional characters, called indicators, are used in some fields to provide the computer with extra information. If indicators are not needed, these areas are left blank. For example:

245 14 $aThe Viking dig :$bexcavations at York /$cRichard Hall.

The first indicator "1" instructs the computer to make an added entry for the title. The second indicator "4" indicates that the first four characters of the title need to be skipped when the title is filed.

Subfields and Subfield Codes

The elements within a field are called subfields. Each subfield is introduced by a subfield code. For example, in the title and statement of responsibility field:

245 14 $aThe Viking dig :$bexcavations at York /$cRichard Hall.

$a introduces the title proper
$b introduces the other title information
$c introduces the statement of responsibility.

EXERCISE 4.4

Look closely at each of the MARC records and answer the following questions.

a.
005 19980622221737.1
008 751017r1975 nyucf b   ooo ceng dcam1
010   75025074 |o353717
020   0060100524|c$7.95
040   cobib|beng|dWaOLN
043   n-us---
050 0 PS129|b.H4 1975
082 00 813/.0876B
245 00 Hell's cartographers :|bsome personal histories of science fiction writers /|cwith contributions
         by Alfred Bester ... [et al.] ; edited by Brian W. Aldiss, Harry Harrison.
260   New York :|bHarper & Row,|cc1975.
300   246 p., [2] leaves of plates :|bports. ;|c21 cm.
504   Includes bibliographies.
600 10 Aldiss, Brian Wilson,|d1925- |vBiography.
650   0 Science fiction, American|xHistory and criticism.
650   0 Authors, American|vBiography.
650   0 Science fiction|xAuthorship.
700 1   Bester, Alfred.
700 1   Harrison, Harry.
700 1   Aldiss, Brian Wilson,|d1925-
935   AAN-9408

i.   What type of material is this?

ii.   What is the title?

iii.   Who is the author?

iv.   Is it illustrated?

v.   Write down the ISBN.

vi.   What is this publication about?

b.

```
001  41467310
003  OCoLC
005  20000612120042.0
007  aj cenzn
008  990506t19961988couag    a   1 eng cem a
010  99441694 /MAPS
020      0925873128
034  1   a|b500000|dW1094500|eW1092700|fN0385200|gN0383400
040      DLC|cDLC|dOCL
049      QUEM
072  7   E63|2|cg
099      917.925 Trails 1996
110  2   Trails Illustrated (Firm)
245  10  Arches National Park, Utah |h[map] /|cNational Geographic Maps, Trails Illustrated.
250      Rev. 1996.
255      Scale ca. 1:50,000 |c(W 109045--W 109027/N 38052--N 38034).
260      Evergreen, Colo. :|bTrails Illustrated, |c[1996], c1988.
300      1 map :|bcol., plastic ;|c69 x 53 cm., folded to 24 x 11 cm.
500      Relief shown by contours and spot heights.
500      Title from panel.
500      "This map is based on USGS topographic maps modified and revised by Trails Illustrated in
         cooperation with the National Park Service ..."
500      Includes text, descriptive indexes to trails and roads, and ancillary "View from southwest".
500      Text and map of "Utah canyon country" on verso.
500      "211."
590      917.925 TRAILS 1996
650  0   Hiking |zUtah |zArches National Park |vMaps.
650  0   Trails |zUtah |zArches National Park |vMaps.
651  0   Arches National Park (Utah) |vMaps, Topographic.
```

i.   What type of material is this?

ii.   What is the title?

iii.   Is it colored or black and white?

iv.   Who produced it?

v.   What is it about?

Reading Catalog Records

EXERCISE 4.5
Look at the following examples of catalog entries and answer the questions.

a.

TITLE	The gentleman's recreation : in four parts, viz. hunting, hawking, fowling, fishing : wherein these ... exercises are largely treated of, and the terms of art for hunting and hawking more amply enlarged ... with an abstract at end of each subject of such laws as relate to the same ... with the addition of a Hunting-horse.
AUTHOR	Cox, Nicholas, fl. 1673-1721.
EDITION	3rd ed.
PUBLISHED	London : printed by Freeman Collins for Nicholas Cox, 1686.
DESCRIPT	4 pts. in 1 v. : 4 plates, ill. ; 19 cm.
SUBJECT	1) Fowling. 2) Hunting. 3) Falconry. 4) Fishing. 5) Forestry law and legislation—Great Britain. 6) Game-laws—Great Britain.
NOTE(S)	Each part has special t.p. and separate pagination.
CONTENTS	With which is bound: G. Langbaine, The hunter. Oxford, 1685.

	LOC'N	CALL #	STATUS
1	Petherick Reading Rm	799.2 COX	Not for loan

i.   What type of material is described in this catalog entry?

ii.   Who is the author?

iii.   Who published this item?

iv.   What is the date of publication?

v.   Which edition is this publication?

vi.   Is it illustrated?

vii.   Does it include an index?

viii.   What is this publication about?

ix.   How could you find other books on this subject?

x.   Which classification scheme does this library use?

xi.   Why do you think this publication cannot be borrowed?

b.

TITLE	The Mind [videorecording] : aging / produced, directed and written by John Heminway.
ADD AUTHOR	Heminway, John.
	WNET (Television station : New York, N.Y.)
	British Broadcasting Corporation.
PHYS DESCR	1 videocassette (VHS) (56 min.) : sd., col. ; 1/2 in.
SUBJECT	Brain—Aging.
	Aging.
	Aged—Diseases.
	Brain—Diseases.
SUMMARY	Explores the effects of aging on the brain, including diseases such as stroke, Alzheimer's and Parkinson's, and asks why some people retain full mental capacity in old age while others deteriorate mentally.
NOTE	Off-air recording. Originally produced: WNET, New York and BBC, 1988.
ALT TITLE	Aging.

	LOC'N	CALL #	STATUS
1	Central library	QP356.4.M53 1988	Available

i.   What type of material is described in this catalog entry?

ii. Who is the author?

iii. Who is the publisher of this item?

iv. What is it about?

v.   What is the playing time?

c.

TITLE	International journal of early childhood = Revue internationale de l'enfance préscolaire = Revista internacional de la infancia pre-escolar.

> LIB. HAS   Vol.1, n.1 (1969) to the present.

PUBLISHER	Dublin, Ireland : OMEP Publications, 1969-
PHYS DESCR	v. : ill. ; 25 cm.
FREQUENCY	Semiannual
NOTE	English, French, or Spanish, with summaries in the other two languages.
SUBJECT	Education, Preschool—Periodicals.
ISBN/ISSN	0020-7187
ADD AUTHOR	World Organization for Early Childhood Education

i.   What type of material is described in this catalog entry?

ii.   When was the first issue of this publication published?

iii.   In what language is it published?

iv.   How would you find other items on the same topic(s)?

EXERCISE 4.6

Answer the following questions using a library of your choice. (Use a large, general library if possible.)

a.   How many items does the library hold by Maurice Sendak?

b.   Does the library hold *Silent spring?* Where?

c.   Does the library have any items on dress design?

d.   How much material does the library hold on Virginia Woolf?

e.   Does the library have anything on International Women's Year? Where?

f.   Does the library subscribe to the popular newsmagazine *Time?* Where would you find it?

g.   Does the library hold any items on practical politics?

h.   How much material can you find on Pierre and Marie Curie?

i.   Does the library have anything on Volvos? Where?

j.   Does the library have any sound recordings of Dame Joan Sutherland? If so, what are they?

EXERCISE 4.7

a.   Which of the following could you look for in your library's catalog and why?

    i.   Does the library receive *Scientific American*?

    ii.   Does the library have a copy of *Travels with Charley*?

    iii.   Is there an article about robots in *Life* magazine?

    iv.   Does the library have any videos on occupational health and safety?

    v.   Where would I find a recent article by Diane Sawyer?

b.   How do you identify the following in your library catalog:

    i.   serials

    ii.   sound recordings

    iii.   microforms

    iv.   CD-ROMs

    v.   pamphlets

c. What name is used in the catalog for:
    i.   Louisa M. Alcott

    ii.   IRS (Internal Revenue Service)

    iii. National Gallery of Modern Art (Italy)

    iv.   American Enterprise Institute

    v.   National Baseball Museum

d. What subject heading(s) are used in the catalog for:
    i.   testing computer software

    ii.   American football games

    iii. serials about stamp collecting

    iv.   the mental health of adolescents

    v.   aid to developing countries

Filing

Most filing, especially in catalogs, is now done automatically. However, it is still important to understand the principles of filing in order to find items in lists, whether they are in print or online. Because information is arranged according to a particular set of filing rules, familiarity with the rules is the most effective approach to locating information in these listings.

Library filing rules have evolved with the developments in automated library systems. When catalog cards were filed manually, the rules allowed for interpretations of the headings to be made. For example, distinctions were made between names and subjects because they were filed in separate sequences: "St." could be filed as if it were spelled "Saint". Now that computers do most of the filing, the rules need to accommodate this much more mechanical approach.

The filing rules for catalog cards were:
- *A. L. A. rules for filing catalog cards*, Chicago, American Library Association, 1942
- *ALA rules for filing catalog cards* 2nd ed., Chicago, American Library Association, 1968.

Many libraries with manual catalogs still file by the 1968 rules because of the time and effort required to change filing practice.

The development of automated systems led to a new set of rules:
- *ALA filing rules*, Chicago, American Library Association, 1980.

These rules provide for the filing of bibliographic records in any format.

Principles of Filing

There are two basic methods of filing entries in a single sequence:
- word by word
- letter by letter.

Using one or other of these methods results in a quite different arrangement. Therefore, you must be able to recognize the basic filing arrangement in order to find a particular entry in a catalog, bibliography, or listing.

Word by Word

Most library materials are filed word by word. That is, each word is filed alphabetically but the space at the end of a word is filed before any letter. This is often referred to as the principle of "Nothing files before something". For example:

    New Australians
    New England cookbook
    New Zealand in colour
    Newbery Medal winners
    Newton and gravity

Letter by Letter

Some works are filed letter by letter. This means that spaces between words are ignored and each letter in each word is filed alphabetically. For example:

New Australians
Newbery Medal winners
New England cookbook
Newton and gravity
New Zealand in colour

ALA Filing Rules (1980)

The rules are intended to apply to the arrangement of bibliographic records regardless of the rules by which the records have been created.

The main rules are summarized below. For any filing situations not covered here, consult the full text of the 1980 *ALA filing rules*.

The basic filing order is word by word.

New Zealand in colour
Newbery Medal winners

The rules use the "file-as-is" principle. File an entry as it looks rather than as it sounds.

Miss Read
Misunderstood in Miami
Mr. Chips

No distinction is made between different types of headings. Therefore, personal names, corporate names, titles, and subject headings are all interfiled in the same sequence.

Archer, Jeffrey
Architects Anonymous
ARCHITECTURE
Architecture and design in Australia

The principle of "nothing before something" applies, so a space (or equivalent) is considered as nothing.

S E C
Sally Kelly

Dashes, hyphens, diagonal slashes, and full stops are all regarded as equivalent to a space or "nothing". However, if any of the above precede the first character in an element, they are ignored.

AAP Reuters
- angry young men
Apres vous

O, Chae-ho
O.E.C.D.
OAU/STRC
OAU today

NORTHEAST COMMUNITY COLLEGE LIBRARY

Upper and lower case letters are equivalent.
>ARCHITECTURE
>Architecture and design
>ARCHITECTURE--FRANCE

All entries beginning with numbers are arranged before entries beginning with letters. Numbers are filed in numerical order.
>16 : Heaven or Hell?
>44 short poems
>101 ways to get a job
>AAP Reuters

Numbers that are spelled out interfile with other entries.
>Ferguson, John
>Fifty-five days in Peking
>Forty-four nursery rhymes
>FRANCE

Punctuation used to increase readability in numbers (e.g., 2,730) is ignored.
Other punctuation (e.g., 1948/49) is treated as a space.
>10/3 a date to remember
>101 uses for a dead cat
>1,001 years in space

Initial articles that are an integral part of personal or place names (e.g., El Greco, Las Vegas) are included in filing.
>Long Island
>Los Angeles
>Louisiana

Initial articles at the **beginning** of title, uniform title, series, and subject entries are ignored.
>West, John
>The West Sports Association
>The western adventure
>A western film

Articles in the middle of a heading are filed in the same way as any other word.
>West is best
>West is better than North
>West is the best

Initials, initialisms, and acronyms are filed as they appear in the entry. If they are written with spaces, dashes, hyphens, diagonal slashes, or periods between letters (e.g., L.A.A., S E C), file each letter as a separate word. If they appear as a word (e.g., NUCOS) or have letters separated by symbols other than those mentioned above (e.g., P*E*R*T*), they are filed as words.
>F.F.B.
>Father Time

Hum and be happy
H*Y*M*A*N K*A*P*L*A*N
Hymns of praise

U.N. or World War III?
Uncontrolled joy
UNESCO
Unicef
United Arab Republic

A prefix that is written as a separate word at the beginning of a personal or place name (e.g., De Alberti) is treated as a separate word.
> Da Ponti
> Dante
> De Alberti
> De La Fontaine
> Dean
> Debrett

A prefix that is joined to the rest of the name directly or by an apostrophe without a space (e.g., D'Arcy, Maclaren) is filed as part of the name.
> Da Trevi
> Daniel
> D'Arcy
> Dastardly deeds in Dundee

With the exception of dashes, hyphens, diagonal slashes, and full stops, and the special rules for numbers, all punctuation and nonalphabetic symbols are ignored in filing.
> $$$ and sense
> Andrew ***, Baron of Styx
> Andrew/Sarah/Eugenie/Beatrice
> Andrew Windsor, the last monarch?
> Andr*w, son of Elizabeth

Exercise 4.8

Examine the list below and ensure that you understand the filing position of each entry. Refer to the above rules for any arrangement you are not sure of.

7 little Australians
10/3 a date to remember
16 : Heaven or Hell?
44 short poems
101 uses for a dead cat
1,001 years in space
AAP Reuters
$$$ and sense
Andrew ***, Baron of Styx
Andrew/Sarah/Eugenie/Beatrice
Andrew Windsor, the last monarch?
Andr*w, son of Elizabeth
- angry young men
Apres vous
Architects Anonymous
Architecture and design in Australia
ARCHITECTURE--FRANCE
Da Ponti
Dante
D'Arcy
Dastardly deeds in Dundee
De Alberti
De La Fontaine
Dean
F.F.B.
Ferguson, John
Fifty-five days in Peking
Forty-four nursery rhymes
FRANCE
Hum and be happy
H*Y*M*A*N K*A*P*L*A*N
Hymns of praise
Long Island
Los Angeles
Louisiana
Mac Donald, John

MACALISTER RIVER
MacAlister, Stephen
Macdonald
Machinery
Mack the knife
McDonald, Peter
Miss Read
Misunderstood in Miami
Mr. Chips
New England cookbook
Newbery Medal winners
O, Chae-ho
O.E.C.D.
OAU/STRC
OAU today
S E C
S.P.C.A.
Sally Kelly
Senatorship
SINGAPORE
* The Society to Outlaw Pornography
Spencer, Andrew
SPUD : let's prevent unwholesome diets
U.N. or World War III?
Uncontrolled joy
UNESCO
Unicef
United Arab Republic
UNITED NATIONS – BIBLIOGRAPHY
The United Nations in the twentieth century
UNITED STATES – THE WEST
The United States under Reagan
THE WEST
West, John
The West Sports Association
A western adventure

EXERCISE 4.9

File the following sets of entries word by word using the 1980 ALA filing rules. If you find this difficult, write each word of the exercise on a separate card. Practice filing the cards until you are confident and then complete the exercises in the book.

a.

Air conditioning

Air cushion vehicles

Airports

Air transport

Air and space resources

Aircraft

Air pollution

Air Force

Airfields

Air, Lesley

b.

English men of literature

England and the near east

Englische dogges

English historical documents

Engines and trains

Englishmen

Engineers unlimited

English literature

The enigma of drug addiction

Englisch Sprechen!

c.

Gone is gone

Go tell it on the mountain

Gold fever

Gondolas of Venose

Golden girls

Good housekeeping

Goody Townhouse

Good wives

Go down Moses

Goannas

Gold and silver

Golf for amateurs

Goodness gracious me

Goodbye cruel world

Gold mining

d.

Boole, George

Booby

Book of common order

Bookplate

Books

Book of the dead

Book scorpion

Book of common prayer

Book lice

Book worm

Booksellers and bookselling

Bookbinding

Book of famous ships

Books that count

Bookish

Book of English essays

Books and reading

Book

e.

Approach to housing

A is for alphabet

Danger on the ski trails

That's the way

The language laboratory

The laundry basket

Label manufacturing

La laine

Le Lagon

An April After

Archaeology and Old Testament

A Lexicon of the German language

Lexicon of jargon

That was summer

La la

Le laboratoire

The labour gang

The labrador puppies

Ladders and snakes

An Approach to Hamlet

That's me

The Acts

The Danger of Equality

The Archaeology of Carajou

f.

Twenty poems

Twenty and two

$12 to May

20% profit

Twelve angry jelly beans

Twenty soldiers

12 x 8 : Paper read to the Crown Club

Twelve drunk teddy bears

20 + 20 = 40

20/- change

g.

14 lbs.

Fourteen equates to ...?

Fourteen likely lads

4 favorite epic poems

Four and forty

14% of a lifetime

14 days of Hell in the Pacific

44 favorite short poems

$14 a day to tour Europe

14 = 10 + 4

EXERCISE 4.10

Here are some of the exercises you have just filed word by word. Now file each set letter by letter.

a.

Air conditioning

Air cushion vehicles

Airports

Air transport

Air and space resources

Aircraft

Air pollution

Air Force

Airfields

Air, Lesley

b.

English men of literature

England and the near east

Englische dogges

English historical documents

Engines and trains

Englishmen

Engineers unlimited

English literature

Enigma of drug addiction

Englisch Sprechen!

c.

Gone is gone

Go tell it on the mountain

Gold fever

Gondolas of Venose

Golden girls

Good housekeeping

Goody Townhouse

Good wives

Go down Moses

Goannas

Gold and silver

Golf for amateurs

Goodness gracious me

Goodbye cruel world

Gold mining

d.

Boole, George

Booby

Book of common order

Bookplate

Books

Book of the dead

Book scorpion

Book of common prayer

Book lice

Book worm

Booksellers and bookselling

Bookbinding

Book of famous ships

Books that count

Bookish

Book of English essays

Books and reading

Book

EXERCISE 4.11

The following lists are in correct alphabetical order. For each list, decide whether the order is word by word, or letter by letter. State briefly how you recognized the order.

a.

Cape Cod Bay
Cape Dyer
Cape Jervis
Capel
Capela de Campo
Capel Curig
Capella, Mt.
Cape Preston
Capetown
Cape Virtue

The order is

I recognized the order by

b.

File extensions
File menu
File - print command
File - save as command
Files - assembling
Files - MIDI
Find program
Find tab (Help program)
Finding - Hidden windows
Floppy discs

The order is

I recognized the order by

c.
C:\⸻⟩ prompt. *See* Dos prompt
CD player
CD-ROM drives
CD-ROM viewing
CD-ROMs. *See* Compact Discs
Control panel
Controls
Ctrl key
Free form select tool
FreeCell

The order is

I recognized the order by

d.
Hawker, R.
Hawker Roofing
Hawker's Barry Butchery
Hawker Self Serve
Hawker Tennis Centre
Hawkes, Adrian J.
Hawkesbury Constructions
Hawkes Butchery
Hawkins, Jimmy
Hawkinson Self Serve

The order is

I recognized the order by

EXERCISE 4.12

Look at the latest edition of your local telephone directory (white pages) and answer the following questions.

a. Does the directory have a section explaining its filing rules? How does it arrange entries so that clients can find what they are looking for?

b. List the elements you think could cause a filing problem (e.g., numbers, or the prefixes Mc and Mac). How does the directory deal with these elements?

c. Is the directory internally consistent; that is, does it actually file entries in a consistent way, as it explained?

EXERCISE 4.13

Use the 1980 filing rules to arrange each of these bibliographies in correct word by word order. Take care to transcribe each citation accurately.

a.

Stumbler, Irwin. *The encyclopedia of pop, rock and soul.* Chicago: St. Martin's Country Music Foundation, 1989.

Manuella, Timothy W. *Rock around the Bloc: a history of rock music in Eastern Europe and the Soviet Union.* Oxford: OUP, 1990.

The music and the musicians: pickers, slickers, cheatin' hearts, and superstars. Chicago: Abbeville, 1988.

St John, A. J. "I knew Elvis", in *Canberra times*, 21 November 1959, p. 6.

Robertson, Fred. *Lissauer's Encyclopedia of popular music in America, 1800 to the present.* New York: Paragon, 1991.

Saint, John. *The Penguin encyclopedia of popular music.* London: Viking, 1989.

Rees, David and Markoff, John. "Led Zeppelin" in *Music and musicians*, No. 54, September 1994, p. 2-7.

Manuel, Peter. *Popular music of the non-Western world: an introductory survey.* Oxford: OUP, 1988.

Rees, Dafydd and Crampton, Luke. *Rock movers and shakers,* Cardiff: ABC-CLIO, 1991.

An encyclopedia of rock. Washington, DC: Schirmer, 1987.

Robinson, D. C. *Music at the margins: popular music and global cultural diversity.* Edinburgh: Sage, 1991.

b.

IEEE transactions on information technology. New York: Institute of Engineers, 1955-

I.T.: journal of information technology. Sydney, Australia: Macquarie University, 1995-

Access: the supplementary index to Internet serials. Washington, DC: Gaylord, 1975-

IEEE transactions on computers. New York: Institute of Electrical and Electronics Engineers, 1959-

IEEE/ACM transactions on networking. New York: Institute of Electrical and Electronics Engineers and the Association for Computing Machinery, 2:2, Winter 1994.

IEEE transactions on communications. New York: Institute of Electrical and Electronics Engineers, 15:8, August 1995.

IEEE annals of the history of computing. Los Alamitos, Calif.: IEEE Computer Society, 1979-

I.T. and accounting: the impact of information technology, edited by Bernard C. Williams and Barry J. Spaul. London: Chapman & Hall, 1991.

I.B.M. journal of research and development. New York: International Business Machines Corporation, 37, 1993.

An accent on periodicals: a survey. Canberra: Library Association of Australia, 1989.

NATO Advanced Study Institute on Information Technology and the Computer Network, *Information technology and the computer network*, edited by Kenneth G. Beauchamp. Berlin: Springer-Verlag, 1984.

Information technology and libraries. Chicago: American Library Association, 17:3, March 1998.

Information sources in information technology, editor, David Haynes. London: Bowker-Saur, 1990.

EXERCISE 4.14

The following list of serials is in correct 1980 filing rules order.

24 hours: ABC FM program

Abridged reader's guide to periodical literature

Booklist

Bulletin of the Centre for Children's Books

CSIRO papers

Defense abstracts

Four to fourteen

The horn book magazine

A journal of documentation

Mt Isa Mines ecological quarterly

Queensland. Dept of Education. Annual report

Sociofile

Interfile the following into the list above.

The bulletin
Mount Morgan mining review
Social science abstracts
Book review digest
4 weekly poets
Defence index
3rd world report
The journal of early childhood behavior
C.S.R. quarterly report
Queensland agricultural review

EXERCISE 4.15

The following catalog entry headings are in correct 1980 filing rules order.

20th Century Britain

114 ways to be your own boss

150 masterpieces of drawing

1050 jewellery designs

1200 Chinese basic characters

1200 notes, quotes, and anecdotes

150,000 years

Oliver, I. J.

Oliver Pty Ltd

One hundred and two H bombs

One single minute

One thing necessary

O'Neill, Fred J.

TV Shopping Network

Twentieth century drama

Interfile the following into the list above.

160,000 kilowatts
One thousand and one fishing trips
1250 years at Westbury
O'Neil's private war
100 ideas for the pianist
Olivers galore
The twentieth century
Twelve lesson course
Twelve noon
One two buckle my shoe
One Australia
106 funny things
T. W. U. report
One thousand and one nights
160 feet down

EXERCISE 4.16 (OPTIONAL)

This exercise is challenging. If you have difficulty, check the answers in the back or consult a teacher or supervisor.

These entries are in order. Examine them and determine which filing principles were used.

150 masterpieces of drawing

114 ways to be your own boss

112 2nd form students

One hundred and two H bombs

One single minute

1050 jewelry designs

'39 to '94: the years of change

3000 elephants in a Mini?

3111 buttons

3001: the year of the future

20th century Britain

Twentieth century drama

The filing principles are:

Now interfile the following.

1001 fishing trips
100 ideas for the pianist
Twelve lesson course
12 noon
The twentieth century
One two buckle my shoe
One Australia
106 funny things
One thousand and one nights
150,000 years
160 feet down
3010 pieces of paper
3101 feet of rope
113 teams of netball players
30 bald heads
100,000 jelly beans in a bag
3001 days to blast off

Chapter 5
OTHER BIBLIOGRAPHIC TOOLS

Introduction
In addition to the library's own catalog, many other bibliographic tools are used to check bibliographic details. In libraries, this checking (usually called bibliographic verification) is important for acquisitions, interlibrary loans, preparing bibliographies for clients, and other reference work.

Increasingly these sources of information are available electronically, a format that is often less expensive to publish and easier to update quickly. Many of the databases used for bibliographic verification are available online and on CD-ROM. Online information is more up-to-date, whereas information on CD-ROM is often easier and cheaper to access.

National Bibliographies
A national bibliography:
- provides a list of publications published in one country or in one language
- includes items received under legal deposit and cataloged by a national agency or by its authorized agencies
- is usually arranged in classified order with detailed indexes.

National Libraries
National libraries collect and preserve the published and unpublished output of a nation, including the publications of its government. The catalog of a national library is usually the best place to find information about the publications of that country.

The Internet locations or Uniform Resource Locators (URLs) are given below for several national libraries:

Library	World Wide Web
National Library of Australia	www.nla.gov.au
National Library of Canada	www.nlc-bnc.ca
British Library	www.bl.uk
Biblioteca Nacional de Venezuela	www.bnv.bib.ve

More examples can be found in lists such as the ones maintained by IFLA (International Federation of Library Associations and Institutions) and the Library of Congress:

Organization	World Wide Web
IFLA	www.ifla.org/II/natlibs.htm
Library of Congress	www.loc.gov/global/library/library.html#national

Library of Congress (LC)

The Library of Congress is the largest library in the world, with a collection of nearly 120 million items representing over 450 languages. The collection includes books, serials, recordings, photographs, maps, and manuscripts. Originally mandated to serve the research and information needs of the members of Congress, LC is viewed as the national library of the United States. In fact, the Library of Congress Internet Resource Page cited above includes four national libraries for the United States:

> Library of Congress
> U.S. National Library of Medicine (NLM)
> U.S. Department of Education Library
> The National Agricultural Library (NAL).

The Library of Congress acquires its materials from:

- mandatory copyright deposit: the publisher or copyright owner of all works published in the United States under copyright protection is required to provide two copies to the copyright office within three months of publication
- materials from other government agencies (local, state, and federal levels)
- gifts
- purchases
- exchanges with libraries in other countries.

LC's online catalog is a database of records that represent and describe the millions of items held in the collection. This catalog is available on the World Wide Web at http://catalog.loc.gov/

Union Catalogs

Union catalogs usually describe the holdings of more than one library (e.g., member libraries of a consortium or regional or state library system). All types of libraries in North America regularly report their holdings to one or more union catalogs. These catalogs include information such as:

- the name or symbol of the library or libraries that own the items
- information about the holdings
- bibliographic descriptions of the items.

One of the main functions of union catalogs is to identify libraries that hold materials requested on interlibrary loan. Because symbols are usually used to represent the holding libraries, searchers also need access to a list of the symbols. One major source of this information is the *OCLC participating institutions* print directory or web version (http://purl.org/oclc/pi).

URLs for several union catalogs are given below:

Union Catalog	World Wide Web
CONSULS (Connecticut State Library Information System)	www.consuls.org
SunLink (Florida public school union catalog)	www.sunlink.ucf.edu
AMICUS (holdings of 500 Canadian libraries including the National Library of Canada)	www.nlc-bnc.ca/amicus/
OCLC WorldCat (see description below)	www.oclc.org/worldcat

OCLC WorldCat

The largest bibliographic utility in the United States, OCLC is a major source of catalog data for libraries around the world. The WorldCat database consists of MARC records contributed by member libraries (over 36,000 libraries representing more than 70 countries). It is both a union catalog and a fee-based resource, since libraries must pay membership dues to search the database.

Library Catalogs on the Internet

With more library catalogs now accessible via the Internet, libraries and individuals use them to locate bibliographic and holdings information. University and school libraries, federal, state, or provincial government, many state departments, and a growing number of special and public libraries are now online.

Online catalogs are searchable in one, and often both, of the following ways:
- via the World Wide Web using a web browser (Netscape or Internet Explorer)
- via Telnet, using Telnet software.

Remember that the Internet is dynamic, and URLs often change. You may need to search for, and substitute, new addresses for any Internet address provided. Useful sources for this information include:

Website	URL
LCweb	lcweb.loc.gov/z3950/
Hytelnet	www.lights.com/hytelnet/
Libweb	sunsite.berkeley.edu/libweb/
Acqweb	acqweb.library.vanderbilt.edu/

EXERCISE 5.1

Answer the following questions using OCLC WorldCat or the Library of Congress catalog.

1. What is *DMG newsletter* about? Who is the publisher? Is it still being published?

2. Who wrote a criticism in English of Margaret Atwood's book *The handmaid's tale*? What is the title?

3. To which series does Mary Jane DeMarr's book about Barbara Kingsolver belong?

4. Find J. Wheeler's book about birds and air pollution. Transcribe the title and statement of responsibility.

5. Write down the full title of the publication STACS 2000.

6. When was John Lennon born? When did he die?

7. What is the full title information for *Los aztecas*? Who published it in 1998? When was it orginally published?

8.   Find a Braille version of *Cloudy with a chance of meatballs*. Who is the author? Who produced the Braille version?

9.   Find the title of a book by Neil Simon.

10.   Find the title of a book about Neil Simon.

EXERCISE 5.2

Use the *OCLC participating institutions* print directory or web version (http://purl.org/oclc/pi) to identify each of the following OCLC symbols. Give the name of the institution and the corresponding NUC symbol.

OCLC Symbol	NUC Symbol	Library
DY3		
NJF		
SSK		
GPG		
IUF		
BIA		

EXERCISE 5.3

Use OCLC WorldCat to find a library that holds each of the following items. If there is more than library, choose one in your city, region, state, or province. If you do not have access to OCLC WorldCat, use a site such as LibDex (http://www.libdex.com/) to find library catalogs in your area.

1. Marcel Desaulniers' *Death by chocolate cakes*

2. The book with the ISBN 0060930535

3. *The complete climber's handbook*

4. A book produced by the U.S. Advisory Council on Violence against Women

5. A book that lists the plants in the University of Georgia Herbarium

EXERCISE 5.4

Use the OCLC UnionLists and/or WorldCat databases to answer the following questions. If you do not have access to OCLC WorldCat, use a site such as LibDex (http://www.libdex.com/) to find library catalogs in your area.

a. What is the full title of a serial called *Women & literature*? Which libraries in Connecticut hold it?

b. When was the *Omni micronutrients* update first published? What is the URL for the online version?

c. When was the first issue of *Chemical abstracts* published?

d. *The journal of supply change management* has changed its title several times. Give at least one of its former titles and ISSNs.

e. What library in Montana holds the *International journal of occupational health & safety*? Is this the most recent title?

f. I have copies of the *Journal of biological psychology*. What university publishes it? What was its previous title?

g. I know *Rolling stone* is American but is there also an Australian edition? If so, do any American libraries have a subscription to it?

h. How many libraries are listed in the OCLC UnionLists database as holding the *Journal of irreproducible results*? What kinds of libraries are included?

i. I know that the Arkansas State University Library used to collect *Education and urban society*. Does it still subscribe to it? Is the journal available online?

j. I used to read the *ALCTS newsletter.* Is it still published? Does Pepperdine University still have all the issues?

EXERCISE 5.5

Answer the following questions using the Library of Congress catalog.

a. Does the Library of Congress hold the *Arizona traveler's handbook*? Is it a monograph or a serial?

b. What is the original Dutch title of Anne Frank's *Diary of a young girl?* What is the date of publication of the most recent copy held at the Library of Congress?

c. Which serial has the ISSN 0004-7686? Has it changed its title?

d.   What is the title of a joint publication of the U.S. Bureau of Land Management and the U.S. Fish and Wildlife Service about Death Valley National Park?

e.   Are there any catalogs published in 1998 about collecting Beanie babies? Give the title and statement of responsibility of each.

f.   List all the titles in the series Reference Librarian that are held by the Library of Congress.

g.   What publications does the Library of Congress hold about the United Farm Workers of America? Give the title and statement of responsibility of each.

h.   What is the most recent edition of Lois Mai Chan's book about Library of Congress Classification held by the Library of Congress? When was it published and what is its call number?

i.   Who published the periodical *George*? What was the date of the first issue?

j.   Give the author and title of the book with the ISBN 031205436X.

EXERCISE 5.6

Find the URL of the online catalog of each of the following libraries. If they are accessible via both the World Wide Web and Telnet, write down the URL of each. For each library also list the access points available—such as the title (main words), title (exact title), etc.

a.   Your State/Provincial library

b.   A public library service in your state or province

c.   A university library in your state or province

d.   A special library in your state or province

EXERCISE 5.7

Use one of the online catalogs located in Exercise 5.6 to answer the following questions. You may need to search more than one to find all the answers. Note the library in which you find each answer.

a.   Give the author and title of a book about Bill Gates.

b.   Can you find a collection of poetry for children about Thanksgiving? Give the title and publisher.

c.   How many books does the library hold by John Grisham. What are they?

d.   Does the library have any books in the NCASI technical bulletin series?

e.   Find a recent collection of Maya Angelou's poetry. Write down the call number.

f.   How many editions of plays by Arthur Miller does the library have? Note which editions include all the plays and which only contain some of them.

g.   Note the titles and authors of two publications about drugs in sport.

h.   Find the title of a periodical about photography.

i.   Does the library hold any New York City maps? Give the titles of two of them and the organizations that produced them.

j.   How many copies of Jane Austen's *Pride and prejudice* does the library have? When was the novel first published?

Trade Bibliographies

Trade bibliographies are intended primarily for book retailers to indicate which books are available for sale (i.e., in print) and to provide the details needed to order them. They do provide fairly reliable information but further bibliographic verification may still be needed.

Trade bibliographies are produced from information supplied by publishers. They include works irrespective of the date of publication, which means that they are a good place to start if you do not know the date of publication. It is important to note that the information may not conform to library cataloging standards.

Each trade bibliography focuses on one form of material: books, periodicals, spoken word cassettes, computer software, videos, and so on. There is also a national or regional emphasis in each publication usually depending on where it is published, although some bibliographies aim (with varying success) to be genuinely international.

As with other bibliographic tools, printed trade bibliographies are now being supplemented, or even replaced, by CD-ROMs and online databases.

EXERCISE 5.8

Here is a list of some of the most widely used trade bibliographies. Locate as many as you can and add them to the table on the following page according to their focus and format.

Books in Print
Books in Print plus
Books in Print Online
Books out of print plus
http://www.globalbooksinprint.com
Whitaker's Books in Print
Global Books in Print on Disc
Forthcoming Books
International Books in Print
SciTech Reference plus
Guide to Microforms in Print
Ulrich's International Periodicals Directory
Ulrich's plus
Ulrichsweb.com
Words on Cassette
The Software Encyclopedia
Microcomputer Software Guide Online
Bowker's Complete Video Directory (print and CD-ROM)
CD-ROMs in Print (print and CD-ROM)
A-V online (CD-ROM and online)
The Multimedia and CD-ROM Directory
Livres disponibles = French books in print
Libros en venta plus = Spanish books in print plus (CD-ROM)

	Books	Periodicals	Non-Book Materials
Print	*e.g., Forthcoming books*		
CD-ROM			
Online			

Arrangement

Trade bibliographies may be arranged differently from one another. In the electronic bibliographic tools that are rapidly replacing hard copy, the arrangement is sometimes difficult to determine. It is important, however, to be familiar with how each tool is arranged, which access points are provided, and how to find the information you need.

Libraries use different tools for bibliographic verification, and more library staff now rely heavily on one CD-ROM such as *Global books in print* and a range of publishers' and vendors' websites.

The following exercises may suggest particular bibliographic tools to which you may not have access. For this reason, a large number of exercises using a variety of tools are included. It is not necessary to complete all the exercises provided.

You do need to examine some common bibliographic tools to determine how they are arranged and how to find the information you require. If you do not have access to the tools mentioned, substitute any trade bibliographies that available to you. Use the exercises as a guide for examining any bibliographic tool.

EXERCISE 5.9

Find a recent print edition from the following list of bibliographic tools:

Books in Print

Whitaker's Books in Print

International Books in Print

Forthcoming Books

Guide to Microforms in Print

Ulrich's International Periodicals Directory

Livres disponibles = French books in print

Words on Cassette

The Software Encyclopedia

Bowker's Complete Video Directory

CD-ROMs in Print

The following pages contain two sets of questions. Try to examine at least two of the hard copy tools listed above. If you have access to more than two titles, photocopy the questions and complete the same examination of them also.

a. Title:

Publisher:

Date of edition you are using:

Country of publication:

Read the preliminary pages and answer the following questions:

i.   What is the purpose of this tool?

ii.   What material does this tool cover? Mention type of material (e.g., books, periodicals, etc.), country of publication, reason for inclusion.

iii.   How is the main body of the tool arranged?

iv.   What indexes are available? Give names.

v.   How are the indexes arranged? (e.g., numerical order, alphabetical order—each index may be arranged differently)

vi.   For indexes in alphabetical order, is this order word by word or letter by letter? How can you tell?

vii.   How does the tool deal with numbers, initials and acronyms, Mc/Mac, St./Saint? Give examples.

viii. What other information is included (e.g., publishers' contact details)?

ix.   How do I find
          An author?

          A title?

          A co-author?

          An illustrator?

          Items on a particular topic?

          A series?

b.   Title:

Publisher:

Date of edition you are using:

Country of publication:

Read the preliminary pages and answer the following questions:
i.   What is the purpose of this tool?

ii.   What material does this tool cover? Mention type of material (e.g., books, periodicals, etc.), country of publication, reason for inclusion.

iii.   How is the main body of the tool arranged?

iv.   What indexes are available? Give names.

v.   How are the indexes arranged? (e.g., numerical order, alphabetical order—each index may be arranged differently)

vi.   For indexes in alphabetical order, is this order word by word or letter by letter? How can you tell?

vii.   How does the tool deal with numbers, initials and acronyms, Mc/Mac, St./Saint? Give examples.

viii.   What other information is included (e.g., publishers' contact details)?

   ix.   How do I find

An author?

A title?

A co-author?

An illustrator?

Items on a particular topic?

A series?

EXERCISE 5.10

Find a recent electronic version from the following list of bibliographic tools:

Libros en venta plus = Spanish books in print plus	The Multimedia and CD-ROM Directory
Books in Print online	A-V online
Ulrich's plus	Ulrichsweb.com
Microcomputer Software Guide Online	Bowker's Complete Video Directory
Global Books in Print on Disc	Books in Print plus

Below are two sets of questions. Try to examine at least two of the electronic tools listed above. If you have access to more than two titles, photocopy the questions and complete the same examination of them.

a.   Title:

Publisher:

Date of edition you are using:

Country of publication:

Read the introduction and answer the following questions:

i.   What is the purpose of this tool?

ii.   What material does this tool cover? Mention type of material (e.g., books, periodicals, etc.), country of publication, reason for inclusion.

iii.   How is the main body of the tool arranged?

iv.   What access points are provided? Give names.

v.   What other information is included (e.g., publishers' contact details)?

vi.   How do I find:
            An author?

            A title?

            A co-author?

            An illustrator?

            Items on a particular topic?

            A series?

b.   Title:

      Publisher:

      Date of edition you are using:

      Country of publication:

      Read the preliminary pages and answer the following questions:
      i.   What is the purpose of this tool?

      ii.   What material does this tool cover? Mention type of material (e.g., books, periodicals, etc.), country of publication, reason for inclusion.

      iii. How is the main body of the tool arranged?

      iv.   What access points are provided? Give names.

v.   What other information is included (e.g., publishers' contact details)?

vi.   How do I find:
            An author?

            A title?

            A co-author?

            An illustrator?

            Items on a particular topic?

            A series?

World Wide Web Sites

Many libraries prefer to check the details of items they want to order on the website of a vendor or publisher. Most major vendors and publishers have a website linked to their database and many provide an online ordering service.

EXERCISE 5.11

Here are some widely used library vendors and publishers and the URLs of their websites.
a.   Check each of the URLs given and amend them if necessary.

b.   Find URLs for the sites that have not been given URLs.

c.   Add other vendors or publishers and their URLS.

d.   Answer the following questions using more than one site if possible. (Each site is organized differently and provides different information.) For each answer, note the vendor.

Vendor	Website
Barnes and Noble	www.barnesandnoble.com
Midwest Library Service	
Amazon.com	www.amazon.com
Blackwells	
Yankee Book Peddler	
Ebsco	www.ebsco.com
Indigo Books	www.chapters.indigo.ca
Elsevier Science	

Addison Wesley Longman	
DocMatrix	www.docmatrix.com.au
Borders	

i.   Who wrote the biography of Robert F. Kennedy that was published in 2000?

ii.   Give the title of one of Daniel Boorstin's books.

iii.   How much does the paperback edition of *Jurassic Park* cost? Is it available on audiocassette?

iv.   How many of Patricia Cornwall's novels are available in paperback in English? List them.

v.   Who is the publisher of the hardcover edition of *Primary colors*?

vi.   Is the *Academic Press dictionary of science and technology* available on CD-ROM for Windows?

vii.   What is the title of a book about the crash of Swissair Flight 111? Give the ISBN.

viii.   List the catalogs that can be ordered from the Ebsco website. Which one of these does a library need to pay for?

EXERCISE 5.12

Answer the following questions using a current trade bibliographic tool. Although the titles of particular tools are suggested at the beginning of each question, the answers may also be found in other tools. Note the source of each answer: e.g., www.globalbooksinprint.com (checked 30/9/00), *Ulrich's international periodicals directory 1999.*

1.   Books in Print plus
        www.amazon.com
        www.chapters.indigo.ca

i.   Who wrote *Custom homes step by step* in the Better Homes and Gardens series? When was it published?

ii.   What does P. D. James write? Has she written her memoirs?

iii.   Write down the title of the series to which *The Make believe mystery* belongs.

iv.   Give the email and Web addresses of the Maryland Historical Society.

v.   Who published *The Celestine prophecy : an adventure*? In what formats is it available?

vi.   What is the ISBN for the book about motorcycle racing written by Ed Youngblood?

vii.   Give the author, title, and edition of the book with the ISBN 0393970760.

viii.   List the titles of the books by Nellie McClung that are still in print.

ix.   Give the postal address and telephone number of Wild Dove Publishing Company.

x.   Who distributes the publications of the American Library Association in Canada?

2.   International Books in Print
Global Books in Print on disc

i.   Who composed *Sonata for piano, no. 3* published by MCA Music Publishing? Who is the distributor? What is the ISBN?

ii.   Give the full title of the book by Witmer and Samuels on life sciences statistics. What is the latest edition?

iii.   Does HarperCollins have an office in India? Give the postal address.

iv.   Who distributes publications of the American Medical Association in Canada? Give the telephone number and web address.

v.   Is the Hite report on the family still in print? What year was it originally published?

3.   Books in Print
       Books in Print plus
       Books in Print Online
       http://www.globalbooksinprint.com
       Whitaker's Books in Print
       Global Books in Print on Disc
       International Books in Print
       www.amazon.com

i.   Has Giscard D'Estaing written a book about international relations?

ii.   What is the title of Quentin Smith's work about the philosophy of language?

iii.   Are any of William Vantuaono's translations still in print?

iv.   Who edited Christopher Marlowe's *Doctor Faustus*, published in 1997?

v.   Who edited *Energy for a habitable world*? Can you still buy it? How much is the paperback edition?

vi.   What is the ISBN of the title *Read my lips: the cultural history of lipstick*?

vii.   Give the full title and subtitle of a collection of Doonesbury cartoons called something like "Read my lips".

viii. What is the most recent edition of Barbara Requa-Clark's *Applied pharmacology for the dental hygienist*?

ix.   Note the postal address, telephone number, fax number, and email address of the Illinois Library Association.

x.   Give the exact title of a book about pacifism published by the University of Toronto Press.

4.   The Multimedia and CD-ROM Directory
       CD-ROMs in print

i.   Find the entry for the company called Photodisc. What is the address of its website? List several of its published titles.

ii.   Who published *Wanna-be a dino finder*? What is the cost? Who is it intended for? Is it Macintosh-compatible?

iii.   Find a CD-ROM of sound effects. Give the title, publisher, and price.

5.   Bowker's Complete Video Directory (CD-ROM or print)

i.   Find some videos produced since 1990 on earthquakes. Give the titles and dates of publication for three of them.

ii.   Give the postal address, telephone, and fax number of Time-Life Video.

6.   Ulrich's International Periodicals Directory
     Ulrich's plus
     Ulrichsweb.com
     www.ebsco.com

i.   When was the Canadian journal *Revue économique* first published? How often does it appear?

ii. Does *Kompass Italia* have summaries in English? What formats is it available in?

iii. Who publishes *Laugh-makers*? How often?

iv. What is the name of the weekly newspaper published in Garrison, North Dakota? What is its circulation?

v.   What is the ISSN of *Journal of human resources*? How much is the subscription?

vi. *Australian industrial digest* has ceased publication. What was the last issue? Are back copies still available?

vii. Which journal has the ISSN 0364-474X? Who publishes it?

EXERCISE 5.13

Search for each of the following names in any bibliographic tool. Identify the term under which the name is found. (This term is called the entry element.)

Name	Entry Element
Liu Yen	_____
Defense Dept.	_____

Vijay Joshi

_____

Chi Do Pham

_____

Hung Sheng

_____

United States Geological Survey

_____

Fletcher Jones Pty Ltd

_____

Oreste Vaccari

_____

Desh Gupta

_____

Ray Charles

_____

Prince Charles

_____

Charles II

_____

Sommai Premchit

_____

Jalal al Ahmad

_____

Omar Khayyam

_____

Saving Bibliographic Details

Most electronic tools enable users to print bibliographic details or to download them onto a floppy or hard disk. Some libraries load the information directly into an online ordering system; others cut and paste the information into their own ordering software or stationery.

EXERCISE 5.14

Find details of the following items in any of the electronic tools discussed in this chapter. Details should include author, title, publisher, ISBN/ISSN, and price (if available). For each item:

a.   Print the complete record
b.   Save the complete record onto a floppy disk.

i.   The 1999 edition of *Birnbaum's Walt Disney World without kids*

ii.   The seventh edition of *Simplified design of concrete structures*

iii.   A book about human resource management in the hospitality industry; ISBN 0-471-11056-6

iv.   The video about Ecuador and the Galapagos Islands

v.   National Vital Statistics report

EXERCISE 5.15

For each of the publications listed, give the following information:

a.   Format—e.g., print, CD-ROM, online
b.   Publisher
c.   Frequency
d.   Subject coverage
e.   Format coverage
f.   Access points

i.   Words on Cassette **OR** Software Encyclopedia

ii.   SciTech Reference plus **OR** Libros en venta plus **OR** Livres disponibles

iii.   Books in Print **OR** Whitaker's Books in Print **OR** Global Books in Print

iv.   www.amazon.com **OR** www.blackwell.com **OR** www.chapters.indigo.ca

v.   Ulrich's international periodicals directory **OR** Ulrich's plus

vi.   Bowker's Complete Video Directory **OR** CD-ROMs in Print

Chapter 6
CIRCULATION SYSTEMS

Introduction
Circulation refers to the process of lending books and other materials to registered borrowers. A circulation system records the lending (check-out) and return (check-in) of the materials. Loan periods are based on the type of material, the level of demand, and the category of borrower.

Circulation systems attempt to match:
- the borrower's identity
- the items on loan
- the date due.

A circulation system should be able to:
- confirm that the borrower is a registered client and is eligible for service
- differentiate between types of borrowers and lend items according to the type of borrower
- keep track of how many items a client has borrowed already and disallow further lending when the maximum is reached
- tell library staff and users when items are on loan and when they are due to be returned
- bring overdue items to the library's attention for recall purposes
- hold circulated items for other borrowers and inform them when the items are available.

Although automated systems do all or most of these functions, most manual systems are a compromise. Only with the use of a great deal of staff time can manual systems handle more than three or four of the above functions.

Sophisticated library software systems include circulation services that enable library clients to help themselves. For example, through the OPAC (Online Public Access Catalog), users can:
- list all the materials they currently have on loan and the related due dates
- extend the loan period for library materials if they are not on hold for someone else
- place a hold on an item already on loan to another client.

Different systems emphasize different outcomes. Libraries with manual systems need to decide which services are more important to them and organize the workflow accordingly.

Circulation work is quite complex and requires a system that can pull together a great deal of information each time an item is borrowed. These requirements differ depending on whether clients visit the circulation desk or log on to the library system from a remote site.

Customer Relations
One of the most important functions of staff on the circulation desk is customer relations. Clients judge libraries on the attitudes and efficiency of desk staff. Their perception of desk staff sometimes determines whether they will return to the library.

Staff should be:

- friendly
- helpful
- impartial
- informative
- but not overwhelming.

Staff should be particularly aware of the importance of treating clients impartially. Bending the rules for one client will result in demands from others for the same treatment. Being harsh with some may lead to a perception of discrimination.

All libraries have rules and policies, but they also tend to have an informal policy on how these rules are applied. Some libraries are strict in the interpretation of rules, and others are more lenient. Your treatment of clients should be consistent with the treatment provided by other staff.

Borrower Registration

Although most public libraries and publicly supported academic libraries in North America allow anyone to use the collection onsite, all libraries require clients to present personal identification and register if they wish to take items offsite. Once registered, the borrower is issued a paper or plastic card and allowed to check out materials. In automated circulation systems, the library cards are barcoded.

Libraries normally restrict the use of their circulation services to certain client groups. For example, a school library serves its staff and students. Libraries may lend to groups outside their client group, but often charge a fee or require a deposit. For example, educational institutions lending to the public often demand a user fee. This category of borrowers is usually called external borrowers.

EXERCISE 6.1

Fill in the table to show the client groups of each type of library.

Type of Library	Client Group
Public library	
School or academic library	
National library	
Special library	

The Registration Procedure

1. Determine whether the client is eligible for membership and for what particular type of membership.
2. Establish whether the client has the necessary proof of eligibility and proper identification.
3. Ensure that the client understands the conditions of membership, such as deposits and fees.
4. Have the client fill in a registration form and transfer the information to the computer or manual register.
5. Provide the client with a card as proof of eligibility to borrow materials.
6. Explain the borrowing limits including:
   - number and type of items
   - loan period
   - fine policy.
7. If available, provide a guide describing the services and/or a list of opening hours.

1. Eligibility for Membership

When the client first requests registration, you must determine if he or she is in one of the eligible client groups. This involves requesting documentation that identifies his or her status and explaining the various categories of borrowers.

Libraries give different borrowing privileges to different types of clients. Certain types of clients may be able to:

- borrow certain kinds of material while others may not (e.g., adults may borrow videos but children may not)
- borrow for different lengths of time (e.g., teachers may borrow serial issues for three weeks and students for one week)
- be exempt from fines while others are not (e.g., senior citizens may be exempt from fines in a public library)
- borrow larger or smaller numbers of items
- renew items more or less often than others
- be given priority for the use of material (e.g., having items recalled from other borrowers when they request them).

For example, a typical educational institution might offer these differing services to clients:

Category	Material type	Borrowing limit	Time limit	Renewals allowed	Fines
Student	monographs reference reserve	5 1 2	14 days overnight 3 hours	2 0 0	$1 per week $5 per day $1 per hour
Staff	monographs reference AV	No limit 2 2	21 days 1 day 7 days	3 0 2	Nil
Staff from other institutions	monographs	2	7 days	1	$1 per week
Community	monographs	2	7 days	1	$1 per week

EXERCISE 6.2

Visit two libraries in your area. Fill in the tables below to show the client groups they serve and the different privileges given to the different client groups.

Library A: _____.

Category	Material type	Borrowing limit	Time limit	Renewals allowed	Fines

Library B: _____.

Category	Material type	Borrowing limit	Time limit	Renewals allowed	Fines

2. Necessary Proof of Eligibility/Identity

Usually, proof of identity is required when a client wants to be registered. Library policy outlines acceptable proof of identification; this may differ for each client group. For example, school libraries often obtain a list of students and staff from administrative records.

And in a typical public library, proof of identification for the various client groups might be:

Client Group	Proof of Identification
Adults	Driver's license Evidence of paying property taxes to the county or municipality Other identification that includes the home address
Children	Parent's or guardian's identification and signature on the registration form
Senior citizens	Same as for adults plus senior's card, health care card, veteran's card, etc.
Special groups such as housebound, disabled, visually impaired	Letter of introduction from doctor, community nurse, etc.
Non-resident adult	Same as for adults

EXERCISE 6.3

Use the chart below to list what might be used as proof of identity in different types of libraries. Or, verify the policies of different libraries in your area.

Type of Library	Proof of Identification
School library	
Academic library	
Special library	

3. Ensure the Client Understands Conditions

Conditions might include limits on the number or type of materials borrowed, or a deposit or nonrefundable fee required before registration is completed.

It is important to ensure that the client understands these conditions. For example, if public clients of a university library are charged a fee, make certain that they are aware it is a non-refundable annual fee. Explain that it is not a deposit that is returnable when clients cancel their membership and that it excludes access to some library materials such as the reserves collection.

4. Registration Form

A registration form collects all necessary information about the client, including name and contact information for correspondence and overdue notices. Often more than one address is requested (e.g., a home address for staff). The client information is then transferred to a register or list. In an automated system, this is called a client's patron record. Registration forms are usually not kept after being transferred to the computer file unless there is a need for a signature proving that the client agrees to certain conditions.

Some libraries with a smaller number of new clients, such as a special library, may not use a form but enter information directly into the system. This shortcut introduces the risk of error in busy libraries.

Example of a Registration Form

CITY PUBLIC LIBRARY CHILDREN'S MEMBERSHIP											
Membership number		X	5	8	1	7	3	8	4	0	0	1

NAME

ADDRESS   ID SEEN

ZIP CODE

DATE OF BIRTH

I undertake to ensure that my child will return borrowed books on time and in good condition. I agree to pay any charges incurred by my child for lost, damaged, or overdue items.

SIGNATURE OF PARENT OR GUARDIAN .... DATE ....

Screens for Registering a Client in an Automated System

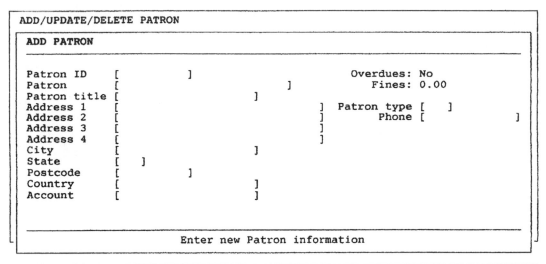

```
ADD/UPDATE/DELETE PATRON
  ADD PATRON

  Patron ID    [              ]                Overdues: No
  Patron       [                     ]            Fines: 0.00
  Patron title [                 ]
  Address 1    [                     ] Patron type [   ]
  Address 2    [                     ]        Phone [              ]
  Address 3    [                     ]
  Address 4    [                     ]
  City         [               ]
  State        [   ]
  Postcode     [         ]
  Country      [               ]
  Account      [               ]

                    Enter new Patron information
```

```
ADD/UPDATE/DELETE PATRON
  ADD PATRON: 1
   ADDITIONAL PATRON INFORMATION

   Date added       [  /  /  ]
   Card expires     [  /  /  ]
   Last transaction [  /  /  ]
   Patron status    [   ]
   Items borrowed   [     0]
   Renewals         [     0]
   Comments         [                            ]
   Letter salutation [                           ]
   Trap message     [                                  ]
   Dependents       [                                  ]

R=Record save                                     E=Edit
```

5. Provide Client with a Card

COASTAL PUBLIC LIBRARY
NON-RESIDENT

X 5 8 1 7 3 8 4 0 0 1

SIGNATURE

This card must be produced before library material can be borrowed.

A borrower's card is given to the client as proof of lending privileges. Many libraries will not provide any service unless the client can produce the card. Other libraries will allow service if the client can prove their identity in some other way.

Cards are barcoded for automated systems. Often they are colorcoded for the different client groups.

6. Explain Borrowing Limits and Services

Ensure that the client understands any borrowing limits as well as the fining policy of the library. Many libraries have a handout for this.

Take advantage of this opportunity to provide a little public relations—an important facet of circulation work. Let the client know about the library's other services and where to ask for assistance. Library clients want to feel confident that your services are accessible and valuable.

7. Provide a Printed Guide to Services

If it is available, provide a guide describing the services and/or a list of opening hours.

Keeping Registration Up to Date

Registration is normally done for a specific period such as one calendar year (January-December) or the academic year (September-August). Clients are then asked to re-register so that their patron records can be checked for accuracy. This may involve repeating the whole process or simply updating contact information.

EXERCISE 6.4

Obtain copies of the following from a library:
- a registration form
- a library card
- a policy showing who is eligible for registration, what identification is required, and the possible categories of borrowers
- library promotional material.

Circulation Services
Lending Items

The purpose of circulation systems is to keep track of the library materials on loan to registered borrowers. The widespread use of automated systems has allowed libraries to be more flexible in lending their collections. For example, automated systems can cope with several categories of clients borrowing different types of material for varying lengths of time. Manual systems are often so labor-intensive that libraries are forced to limit the number and types of items that clients may borrow.

Sometimes a client's loan request is not permitted. The client may already have the maximum number of loans allowed or has asked for a type of material that cannot be loaned out. It is very important that all staff follow the policy of the library. If you forbid a loan, give the reason politely: "I'm sorry but students are not allowed to borrow videos." Follow the library's loan policy and be consistent.

Renewals

Libraries expect clients who wish to use items for longer than the loan period to renew the loan. Loans are normally extended unless another client has asked for the material. There may be a limit on the number of times a renewal is allowed to ensure that materials in demand are shared.

Fines

Many libraries impose fines when clients do not return material at the end of the loan period. Fines are used as an incentive to return items in order to make the collection available to as many people as possible.

On the other hand, fines can be a deterrent to returning material, or even to borrowing at all. Dealing with fines requires tact.

Reserves

Library materials that are in high demand are often shelved separately and lent out for shorter periods. For example, material selected by teachers for their students is generally put "on reserve".

Hold

Library users might request that an item on loan be made available to them when it is returned. When the item is returned, an automated circulation system alerts staff that the item is on hold and the client is then notified.

Missing Items

Items that disappear, as well as items that borrowers insist they have returned, must be shown as missing in the catalog. Most (but not all) automated systems remove the "missing" tag automatically when the item is returned or loaned out.

Banning

When clients persistently neglect to return items, refuse to pay for missing items, or have a large number of fines outstanding, they may be banned from using the library's collection. Banning is more common in academic libraries where it is vital that all students have equal access to collections. Banning is a last resort in most libraries, as it is considered bad public relations.

Using an Automated Circulation System

Automated systems vary, but some procedures are common to all of them.

The first task of the day is usually to log on to the computer system. Most have passwords that restrict access to particular parts of the system (often called modules) according to a person's duties. For example, a circulation assistant might be allowed to search the catalog but not to change anything in the records. Passwords should be kept secret and changed frequently in order to protect the system against unauthorized usage.

In a large library, the computer terminals are usually dedicated to a particular function or task. Terminals in the reference area are primarily used to search the OPAC, whereas in the technical services department, they are used for the acquisitions and cataloging processes. In the circulation department, often one or more terminals is permanently used for lending while a second group is used for returns, inquiries, and other tasks such as overdues.

A barcode reader can be used to scan library cards and items with barcodes. The system then links the records and calculates a date due, based on the type of material and/or type of borrower. When items are returned, scanning the item barcode discharges the loan.

Barcode readers, particularly light pens, are notorious for not reading the number every time. Often they still give a finishing "beep", and it is easy to think the number has been accepted. Items are then left unrecorded, or recorded as overdue, when they are actually on the shelves. **When using a barcode reader, always check the screen to be sure that the item's loan or return has registered properly.**

Many libraries provide clients with a system-generated receipt that shows the date due. Others manually stamp a date due slip inserted in the item to provide this information. Some libraries save time by not using date due stamps but do allow clients to stamp their own slips if so desired.

Most systems allow the circulation staff to decide whether illegal loans are to be allowed, rather than just refusing to process the loan. This decision process is referred to as overriding the system.

Some systems use function keys to provide shortcuts from one task to another. It can be timeconsuming for staff to have to move from one task to another by using menu commands only. Learning shortcut keys and functions is an important part of using an automated system efficiently. Some older systems have commands barcoded to allow quick movement from one process to another.

Circulation systems usually calculate fines upon return of the item and generally are able to print a receipt automatically when the fine has been paid. For accounting purposes, or to record proof of payment, these systems also might keep track of the fines paid by each borrower as well as the total of the fines collected.

Exercise 6.5

Practice using a circulation system:
1. Register a new borrower.
2. Lend him or her an item.
3. Discharge the item.
4. Place a hold on an item already on loan for a client.
5. Return the item on hold and notify the client who requested the reserve.
6. Return an overdue item. (Inform the client of the fine, collect the fine, and record payment on the system.)

When you can do this without error, create a list of all the necessary steps in the correct order. Give your list to a coworker to review the procedure.

EXERCISE 6.6

Make a list of the shortcut functions available on the circulation system. You may need to look at the system manual to find them. Type the list and make it available near the loan terminal.

Self-Checkout

Many libraries use self-checkout stations to save staff time checking out material and to reduce lines at the circulation desk. Clients position their barcoded library card and the barcodes of the items they wish to borrow under a barcode reader. The system then records the loans and desensitizes the security strips in the items. Clients who are ineligible to borrow for any reason will be referred to the staff at the circulation desk.

Some drawbacks to the use of self-checkout stations include:

- Automatic checkout may not be effective if barcodes and security strips are not positioned in the same place on all items.
- Libraries intending to introduce self-checkout may have to re-barcode some or all of their collections.
- The desensitizing machine can damage videos and software so they cannot be circulated this way.

Security Systems

Security systems are used to prevent material from being removed from the library without being properly checked out. Items have a magnetic strip placed inconspicuously in them. When the item is checked out, the strip is demagnetized as part of the process. If the strip has not been demagnetized, an alarm rings when the item passes between detection gates or barriers that are usually located near the exit. Strips are remagnetized when the item is returned.

Some libraries pass the item around the barrier without demagnetizing the strips to save time and the expense of a demagnetizer. Clients collect the items when they have passed through the barrier. This can cause problems when the books are taken into other libraries or brought back into the lending library.

If the alarm is activated, do not assume that the client is stealing. Clothing tags, cell phones, items from other libraries, or security strips that have not been properly demagnetized might trigger alarms.

In the event of the alarm going off, here is a procedure to follow:

- Ask the client if he or she has any material from another library or is carrying something else that might have triggered the alarm.
- Politely request to check bags. (The client should open the bags, and staff should just observe.)
- Look for items that might have set off the alarm.
- Confirm that items from your own library are checked out and demagnetized.
- Explain that you may need to pass the material around the gate if, for example, it comes from another library that does not demagnetize items.
- Call for a supervisor if the client refuses to cooperate.

EXERCISE 6.7

List the questions you would ask if a client set off the alarm on the security gate in your library. Practice asking these questions with a coworker.

REVISION QUIZ 6.8

1. Why do libraries distinguish among different categories of borrowers?

2. When do libraries keep the registration card that is filled in by the borrower?

3. What is a "hold"? Choose the correct answer.
   a. The library agrees to keep a book from the shelves until the client picks it up.
   b. The library keeps a book for another client when it is returned from loan.
   c. The library agrees to send a new book to a client when it is processed.
   d. The library puts a book into a special collection because it is in demand and only lends it for a short period.

4. Why is the attitude of circulation staff toward clients so important?

5.   When using an automated system to check out material, you are often given the choice of printing a receipt for all the items loaned out. What is the purpose of this slip?

6.   Under what circumstances would a library consider rebarcoding some or all of the collection?

7.   When would a borrower ask for a renewal?

8.   Why do libraries fine clients for having items overdue?

Reserves

Also called short loan, reserve collections are primarily used in academic or school libraries where several clients want the same material at the same time. Required reading for a course or information needed to complete a particular assignment is often put on reserve.

Many university libraries have a separate short loan or reserve section in their libraries. Often material on short loan is not to be taken outside of the library.

In an academic library, reserve collections usually feature:
- loan periods as short as one day, or even just two hours
- material from the library's collection, personal copies from faculty, and temporary material such as photocopies
- heavy fines to discourage clients from keeping the item longer than permitted, thus disadvantaging others
- strict penalties if fines are not paid (e.g., withholding grades).

Special and public libraries may also have small collections of high-demand materials that are kept behind the service desk so that their use can be monitored.

Material for Reserve

In academic and school libraries, lecturers or teachers normally notify the library about what needs to be placed on reserve. Sometimes all material on reading lists is automatically put here. To manage a reserve collection effectively, it is important to communicate with the teaching staff about their requirements and to ensure that library staff have enough time to process materials and make them available for circulation.

When the library does not have the material in the collection, teachers and lecturers might put their own copies on reserve to make them available to students.

Articles might be obtained via interlibrary loan for reserve collections. Lecture notes and recordings are also often kept on reserve.

In nonacademic libraries, material is generally put on reserve by library staff when they anticipate high demand.

Adding Material to Reserve Collections

Material in the library collection is put on reserve by:

- moving or copying the item record to the reserve system
- specifying the course for which the item has been put on reserve
- changing the call number in the item record and on the item itself to include the collection symbol
- reshelving the material in a separate section of the library.

Material being added to the reserve collection is normally marked with large stickers or distinctive book jackets for easy identification by circulation staff.

For materials that are not part of the library collection, a temporary item record is created. Most automated circulation systems allow you to do this without having to add a full bibliographic record to the catalog.

Information on the relevant course is added to the record to allow staff to locate items that are requested by course name or number, or by the name of the lecturer. Students often do not have the citations of material they require; they only know that some material has been placed in the library for them.

Reserve Loans and Bookings

Varying loan periods can confuse staff and clients. To avoid this, many libraries offer only a few choices, such as two-hour, four-hour, or overnight loans. This policy also depends on the flexibility of the booking system.

Many booking systems allow students to reserve material ahead in order to use it at particular times. This is done to give part-time students the same opportunity to access material as full-time students.

If items are not returned to the reserve desk on time, another client is disadvantaged, so fines are heavy and no grace period is allowed. As with other library fines, grades are often withheld until fines are paid completely.

In public and special libraries, material on reserve is often only available on overnight loan or for use in the library only. This ensures that all clients have an equal opportunity to use the material.

The screen display below shows two short loans and two bookings.

```
RESERVE FUNCTIONS                                              11:41:32

Time slot          Patron ID/Patron                 Out     In

09:00 - 11:00 |  456/K. SMITH                    | 09:08 | 10:39
11:00 - 13:00 |  678/JAMES BROWN                 | 11:39 |
13:00 - 15:00 |  68/FRED SMITH                   |       |
15:00 - 17:00 |  8241X/DAVID JONES               |       |




Reserve date: 23/09/98
ID number: SL005
Title: SHARES

R=Reserve          O=Check Out                B=Backward
S=Search                                                    ESC=Exit
```

EXERCISE 6.9

Consider a library where you are familiar with the short loan or reserve section.

List the issues for library staff in managing such a collection.

List the issues for library clients in using such a collection.

REVISION QUIZ 6.10

1. Why do libraries set up special short loan or reserve sections?

2. Name three differences between short loan conditions and normal loan conditions.

3. Where do the materials on reserve come from?

4. What types of libraries use a reserve system?

Chapter 7
COLLECTION MAINTENANCE

What Is Collection Maintenance?

In order to provide an efficient service to users, libraries need to maintain and preserve their collections. Library staff keep library materials in usable condition and follow certain storage and shelving practices so that the materials stay that way.

Collection maintenance involves the following tasks:

- **Final processing**: the physical preparation of library materials for inclusion in the collection. This may involve covering or strengthening them or protecting them by placement in boxes or folders.
- **Storage**: different materials require different storage methods. The materials in a library vary greatly in kind, size, and shape (e.g., atlases, maps, books, pamphlets, videos, and films).
- **Shelving**: placing new materials on the shelves or replacing items after use.
- **Care of the collection**: providing the correct environment for the materials, checking their physical condition, and repairing damaged materials.
- **Inventory and shelf reading**: checking the order of material on shelves.

Collection maintenance is important because:

- Library materials are often expensive or impossible to replace.
- Materials should be kept in good condition and correct order to make sure that they are accessible and ready to use.
- Users are more inclined to use materials that are in good condition and tend to avoid shabby or damaged materials.

Processing

All items should be cataloged and classified before they are added to the library collection and should be processed to make them ready for use.

Processing is usually divided into two stages:

1. Materials Receipt

There are processing tasks that are carried out when the item is first received and before it is cataloged and classified. These tasks include:

Checking

When an item is received, it must be checked carefully to make sure that it is the item requested and that it is in good physical order. For example, ensure that a book has all of its pages or a kit has all of its parts.

Ownership Marks

Ownership marks are used to show that the item is the property of the library. In the case of books, this mark may be made in a number of places—usually on the verso of the title page and on other designated pages throughout the book. If an item is rare or valuable, ownership marks are not used on the item itself.

Accessioning

Each item is given a unique identifying number called an accession number. This is usually a running number. An accessions register may be maintained although automated systems make this unnecessary. The accessions register shows how many items have been acquired since the collection began. Each number is unique regardless of how many copies of an item are in the library.

Barcodes are now commonly used as accession numbers. Barcodes do not need to be consecutive for computers to generate the information on the number of items in the collection. (A barcode number is still unique to an item.)

2. Final Processing

The tasks that are completed after the item has been cataloged and classified include:

Call Numbers

A call number is assigned to an item when it is cataloged. The call number, which is usually made up of a classification number and a book number (or letters), determines the item's shelf location. It may also include the physical location such as a branch library or a special collection (e.g., the reference collection). It may also provide a copy number (e.g., Copy 2). For books, the call number may be written on the verso of the title page or on the last page. A spine label with the call number is attached to the cover.

Circulation Stationery

If used, this usually consists of a date due slip, a bookcard, and a pocket for manual circulation systems. Circulation stationery may be attached to the first or last page of the item to provide a flat surface for stamping the due date.

Security

Magnetic security strips (tattle tape) may be inserted as part of a library's security system. These strips are desensitized at the time of borrowing and resensitized on their return.

Covering

A plastic jacket or adhesive cover strengthens a book and protects against soiling. With the exception of adhesive covering, the covering should be attached in such a way that it can be removed for re-covering in future.

Strengthening Strips

Vinyl tape or adhesive covering strips may be used to strengthen weak book bindings. Corners may also be strengthened in this way.

Special Symbols

- **Locations:** some items are sent to branch libraries or special collections and need specific identification. Often color codes are used to indicate different locations if this information is not included in the call number.
- **Type of material:** location symbols are also used for various categories of materials such as serials and audiovisual items.

- **Circulation information:** symbols may be used to indicate circulation information. For example, a red dot may indicate that an item cannot be borrowed.

Final Check

The item must be checked to make sure that all of the processing stages have been completed before it can be shelved ready for patron use.

EXERCISE 7.1

Visit a library and examine an example of each format listed below. Look at the method used to process the item and fill in the table.

	Printed book	Serial	Film	Map	Kit	Video
Where is the library's ownership stamp located?						
Can you find a barcode on the item?						
Is the accession number recorded in the item? If so, where?						
Where is the call number recorded on the item?						
Does the item include circulation stationery? If so, describe it.						
Does the item include security strips?						
Does the item have a cover or special packaging?						
Are there any special symbols on the item such as a sticker to indicate reference?						

Library Suppliers

Libraries purchase the materials needed to maintain and preserve their materials from library suppliers including:

Brodart (http://www.brodart.com)
U.S. Customers:
Brodart Order Center
P.O. Box 3037
Williamsport, PA   17705
Telephone: 1-888-820-4377
Fax: 1-800-283-6087
Email: supplies.customerservice@brodart.com

Canadian Customers:
Brodart Canada Ltd., Order Centre
109 Roy Boulevard
Brantford, ON   N3R 7K1
Telephone: 1-800-265-8470
Fax: 1-800-233-8467
Email: brodart@on.aibn.com

International Customers:
Telephone: 1-570-769-3265
Fax: 1-570-769-5111
Email: supplies.international@brodart.com

Demco (http://www.demco.com)
P.O. Box 7488
Madison, WI   53707
Telephone: 1-800-356-1200
Fax: 1-800-245-1359
Email: order@demco.com

Gaylord (http://www.gaylord.com)
Gaylord Brothers
P.O. Box 4901
Syracuse, NY   13221-4901
Telephone: 1-800-448-6160
Fax: 1-800-272-3412

Canadian Customers:
Telephone: 1-800-841-5854
Fax: 1-800-615-3779

International Customers:
Telephone: 1-315-457-5070 ext. 287
Fax: 1-315-453-5030

Vernon (http://vernlib.com)
2851 Cole Court
Norcross, GA   30071
Telephone: 1-800-878-0253
Fax: 1-800-466-1165
Email: vernon@vernlib.com

EXERCISE 7.2

Using a library supplier's catalog, look at the products that can be used to process library materials. Compare two different formats (e.g., videos and maps) and fill in the table.

	Format 1	Format 2
What products are available in the catalog?		
How much do the products cost?		
Do the products vary from those you saw in the library?		
Suggest reasons the library chose its methods.		

EXERCISE 7.3

Find a book that needs processing and complete the following steps:

1. Apply the ownership stamp:
    - one stamp on the verso of the title page
    - one stamp approximately halfway through the item
    - one stamp on the inside of the back cover.

2. Apply a barcode to the top of the endpaper opposite the back cover in the center.

3. Write the barcode or accession number within the ownership stamp on the verso of the title page.

4. Write the call number in pencil within the ownership stamp on the verso of the title page.

5. Apply tattle tape
    - hardback: place one-sided tattle tape down the spine
    - paperback: place double-sided tattle tape between two pages.

6. Glue circulation stationery to the endpaper opposite the back cover.

7. Make a call number label: for example

    023.0994
    CAT

8. Apply a call number label on the spine if the book is 1.5 cm. or thicker, positioning it 1.5 cm. from the base of the spine. For narrower items, place label on lower front cover, 1 cm. from the bottom edge and 1 cm. from the spine.

9. Apply a location symbol above the call number label if required.

10. Check that all stages have been completed and ask an experienced staff member to review your work.

EXERCISE 7.4

Answer the following questions about the processing exercise.

1. Were the instructions easy to follow?

2. Can you suggest ways to improve the instructions?

3. Could you use these instructions when processing other formats of library materials?

EXERCISE 7.5

Using a library supplier's catalog, list the products used to cover books.

Look at a video on covering books (e.g., Demco's *Protecting library materials from wear and tear*) or read the instructions in a manual (e.g., Schechter's *Basic book repair methods*).

Cover a paperback book, a hardback book, and a book with a dustjacket using the appropriate covering.

Remember to:
- use the materials as economically as possible
- handle the items with care
- keep your work area tidy.

Storage of Library Materials

Introduction

The basic aim of a library is to provide information for its users. To do this, the library must obtain, organize, make available, and preserve the print and non-print materials required to meet users' needs. Libraries collect a range of materials that vary in kind, size, and shape as well as ones that may require special storage.

Choosing the correct form of storage for each format is important in order to ensure that all items remain in good condition.

The storage method chosen for particular materials depends on the following factors:

- cost
- appearance
- the space available
- the library's clientele
- the need to prevent damage to materials
- staffing levels
- the rarity of the materials
- the special needs of specific formats.

Different Formats

Most libraries have separate sequences of shelving to house different sizes and formats of materials. They generally use adjustable shelving to cater for these different requirements. If all materials are shelved together, the library has to allow the maximum height on each shelf. This takes up a lot of extra space.

Printed Books

Most books are stored on bookshelves with book supports to keep them upright. They should not be shelved too tightly because they are likely to be damaged when users try to remove them. Although books can withstand frequent handling before needing repair or rebinding, some libraries cover books to prolong their life. Paperback books may be stored in wire bookracks for ease of access. Large books should be stored horizontally on shelves, but if several are piled on top of each other, the weight causes damage.

Manuscripts and Typescripts

Rare or valuable manuscripts may need to be stored in a secure area such as a locked storeroom or cupboard. If they are on flat sheets, manuscripts may be bound into books, filed in loose-leaf folders, or stored in boxes. Rolled manuscripts are stored in cylinders. Typescripts are handled in the same way.

Pamphlets

These are usually stored in pamphlet boxes on shelves. Some libraries store them in filing cabinets or place them in stiff covers and shelve them upright with the main collection of books.

Pamphlet boxes protect the materials, and users find them easy to handle, but the thickness of the boxes takes up extra space on the shelves. A filing cabinet for pamphlets protects them from light and dust, but the cabinet takes up floor space.

Periodicals

Most libraries display current issues of periodicals on racks that hold the items rigid. Some use transparent plastic covers to protect the issues. Back runs of periodicals may be bound and shelved in the same way as books. Unbound back issues of periodicals are usually stored in pamphlet boxes. Some libraries microcopy back runs or buy microform copies to save space and preserve information.

Maps, Plans, and Diagrams

These formats are best stored flat in plan cabinets, but some libraries roll and store them in plastic, metal, or cardboard cylinders placed in pigeon-hole racks. If they are fragile, they should be interleaved with acid-free paper. Frequently used items may be laminated.

Pictures

Drawings and photographs may be stored in folders in a filing cabinet or mounted in albums. Another option is to use archive boxes that protect the items from light and dust.

Newspapers and Newspaper Cuttings

Recent issues of newspapers are often stored in a hanging file. Older issues may be bound and stored horizontally on specially designed shelving. Some libraries store older issues in archive boxes or shrink-wrap their newspapers. Newspaper cuttings are usually clipped and stored in filing cabinets or shallow drawers. Because newsprint deteriorates quickly, many libraries preserve the information by microcopying newspapers or by purchasing microform copies. More recently, much of this material is being scanned or digitized and made available electronically.

Microforms

Microfiche may be stored in envelopes, boxes, or slotted plastic panels. Microfilm is usually stored in small reels in cardboard boxes that are housed in special cabinets.

Films and Slides

Roll film is best stored in metal canisters. Filmstrips may be stored in boxes. Slides are usually housed in slotted drawers or in transparent plastic sleeves.

Videotapes

Videotapes are usually stored on shelves. They can stand upright and their outer casing is strong enough to protect them from damage. Some libraries use video stands.

Sound Recordings

Compact discs (CDs) may be stored on display racks, in a tower, or on shelves. Cassette tapes are usually stored in cases or drawers or shelved in casings similar to video containers.

Computer Software

Diskettes are usually stored in boxes in order to protect them from light and dust.

EXERCISE 7.6

Visit a library and identify as many formats of material as possible using the list in the table below. Take note of how the materials are stored and fill in the details.

Type of Material	Is it held in the library?	Storage Methods
Printed books		
Manuscripts, typescripts		
Pamphlets		
Periodicals		
Maps, plans, diagrams		
Pictures		
Newspapers		
Newspaper cuttings		
Microform		
Films and slides		
Videotapes		
Sound recordings		
Computer software		

EXERCISE 7.7

Examine a library supplier's catalog and identify the types of equipment and materials available for storing the library materials listed in Exercise 7.6.

Choose **two** formats of library materials—one print and one non-print—and compare the way in which they are stored in a library with the methods of storage shown in the supplier's catalog. Take into consideration the reasons the library chose its method of storage. State which method you think is the most effective.

	Print Format	Non-Print Format
Material		
Storage method used in library		
One storage method suggested in supplier's catalog		
Reasons library chose its method		
Effectiveness of chosen method		

EXERCISE 7.8

Based on your observations in a library, describe three examples of storage methods that may cause problems for library materials and for users. Suggest solutions to these problems.

	Example 1	Example 2	Example 3
Methods that cause problems for materials			
Possible solutions to problems			
Methods that cause problems for users			
Possible solutions to problems			

REVISION QUIZ 7.9

1. Why is it important to maintain a library's collection?

2. What is a spine label?

3. Why do libraries cover books?

4. What is meant by final processing?

5. Name three factors that will affect the storage methods chosen by a library.

Chapter 8
SHELVING

Introduction
The ideal situation in a library is to shelve all the information on a particular topic together in order to make maximum use of all materials. In many libraries, however, the varied formats of library materials, the need for security, a shortage of shelf space, and the costs involved in processing materials lead to the physical segregation of different types of material.

The physical segregation of material may alter usage patterns and the demand for materials. Each library needs to consider its own circumstances and user needs. There is no arrangement that can be applied universally.

Different Shelving Arrangements

Access
Closed Access
This arrangement does not allow the library user to collect materials directly from the shelves, so staff must be available to do this. Sometimes the collections are in accession number order rather than arranged by subject.

Open Access
With this arrangement users can browse and retrieve materials from the shelves. Most libraries are open access and arranged by subject to make browsing possible.

Factors to Consider in Making the Choice between Closed and Open Access
Libraries base this decision on a number of factors, including:
- the nature of the collection (whether the material is up-to-date or archival)
- the size of the collection and the accommodation available
- the need to avoid damage caused by handling
- the availability of staff to service the collection
- the cost and difficulty of replacing items
- the availability and location of equipment necessary to use an item
- the need to preserve the privacy of the material.

It is common for parts of a collection to be closed access, while other sections are open access. Closed access areas may include non-print materials, reserve and high-demand collections, archives, manuscripts, and rare books.

Location
Fixed Location

If the collection is closed access, the items can be shelved in a fixed location. Advantages and disadvantages of this arrangement include:

- Items are shelved in a prescribed place, and new items are added at the end of the sequence. For identification, items are given a running number or accession number (e.g., 7834, 7835, and so on). This way an item stays in one spot in relation to other items.
- Browsing is impossible because there is no subject order. Access is through a catalog or finding aid.
- This system is mainly used for storage areas such as rare book collections or government records and documents.
- Space is used more economically.
- The collection does not need to be reshelved as frequently.
- There is less wear and tear on items.

Relative Location

Most libraries shelve their materials in a relative location, thus allowing users to browse items on the shelves. Advantages and disadvantages of this arrangement include:

- Items are generally arranged using the Dewey Decimal Classification (DDC) or the Library of Congress Classification (LCC) schemes that group materials by subject.
- New items are interfiled with old ones. As the collection expands, an item may be moved along the shelves, but it remains in the same position relative to other items.
- An expanding collection can be difficult to manage because new material must be intershelved. This leads to constant respacing and the resulting costs.

Integration

In addition to decisions about the kind of access and location, library staff also need to decide whether to integrate or segregate sections of the collection.

Total Integration (or Intershelving)

All library materials, regardless of format, are shelved in one sequence. This is the ideal arrangement for a browsing collection.

Nonintegrated Shelving

All formats of material are stored separately according to their space and equipment requirements. This is not as suitable for a browsing collection as is intershelving.

Partial Integration

Some materials are shelved together, especially if they share a similar format, while others are shelved separately. This is the most common option used in libraries and does allow browsing, but users need to be aware that there are other sequences.

Possible Arrangements

Parts of the collection may be arranged:

- by format (e.g., all videos shelved together in one sequence, oversize books on any subject shelved together)
- in alphabetical order (e.g., fiction books arranged alphabetically by author, serials alphabetically by title)
- in numerical order (e.g., volumes within sets, class-together series)
- in classification number order (e.g., DDC, LCC)
- by audience (e.g., young adults, graduate students)
- by lending conditions (e.g., regular circulation, reserve, noncirculating)
- by type of print (large print, braille).

EXERCISE 8.1

Arrange the following examples of fiction books in alphabetical order by author (and by title when there is more than one book by an author). Write the call numbers in the spaces below.

F/TRO	Trollope, Joanna *The men and the boys.*
F/ARC	Archer, Jeffrey *Honour among thieves.*
F/MCC	McCullough, Colleen *The grass crown.*
F/RUS	Rushdie, Salman *The Moor's last sigh.*
F/THE	Theroux, Paul *My other life.*
F/TRO	Trollope, Joanna *Next of kin.*
F/KOC	Koch, Christopher *Highways to a war.*
F/GRI	Grisham John *The client.*
F/KOC	Koch, Christopher *The year of living dangerously.*
F/THE	Theroux, Paul *The happy isles of Oceania.*

1.	2.	3.	4.	5.
6.	7.	8.	9.	10.

Classification Schemes

Classification

In addition to arranging some of the collection by use or format, most libraries use a classification system based on subject for all or most nonfiction material. It helps the client locate an item when the call number (based on a classification scheme) is known and find all items on one subject together.

Dewey Decimal Classification and Library of Congress Classification are the best known and most widely used classification schemes. Sometimes special libraries use other schemes that are more suited to arranging information for their specific client needs.

Dewey Decimal Classification (DDC)

DDC divides all human knowledge into ten main classes using a minimum of three digits followed by a decimal point and further digits if necessary.

The main classes are:

000	Generalities
100	Philosophy & psychology
200	Religion
300	Social sciences
400	Language
500	Natural sciences & mathematics
600	Technology (Applied sciences)
700	The arts
800	Literature and rhetoric
900	Geography and history

This is the most widely used scheme in North America, particularly in public and school libraries. Many libraries use DDC because:

- The decimal notation is simple to assign, shelve, remember, and find.
- The scheme is revised periodically to accommodate new topics.
- Widespread use of DDC and computer technology make it possible for libraries to share the work of classifying.

The DDC number represents the subject. DDC numbers are placed on the shelves in numerical order, grouping similar topics together. The digits following the decimal point are treated as decimal fractions, as illustrated below:

629
629.1
629.12
629.13
629.13092
629.132
629.1323
629.132322
629.133
629.19
629.2
629.201
629.91
629.99
630

Call Numbers

Call numbers are a combination of a DDC number plus a book number or Cutter.

Call numbers based on DDC are usually a combination of numbers and alphabetic symbols. Frequently, libraries add the first three letters of an author's name to a DDC number to create the call number:

629.13 HAN	(Author John Hanson)
629.133 THO	(Author Fay Thompson)
658.4 KEN	(Author Brian Kennedy)
658.403 BRO	(Author Amy Brown)

Optionally, libraries can use the Cutter-Sanborn tables to create a unique call number for each item and to simplify alphabetic arrangement. Cutter-Sanborn numbers consist of the first letter of the author's name followed by numbers taken from the tables to indicate that name. Detailed instructions on how to create these numbers are included in the front of the Cutter-Sanborn tables. Using the examples above, if a library used the Cutter-Sanborn tables, the call numbers would be:

629.13 H251
629.133 T471
658.4 K35
658.403 B877

Call numbers can also indicate the location if needed (e.g., a branch of the library), a special collection to which an item belongs (e.g., reference, audiovisual), and a copy number if there is more than one. For example:

CITY 629.133 THO
REF 629.13 HAN
629.133 T471 c.3

EXERCISE 8.2

Arrange the Dewey Decimal Classification call numbers given below in numerical order. Write the numbers in the boxes.

a.

| 428 | 944 | 808.02 | 822.3 |
| FRO | LAN | ESS | CRE |

| 025.1 | 331.12 | 940.28 | 302.2 |
| ORG | LIF | IND | COM |

| 796.46 | 882.01 | 959.86 | 004.1 |
| ATL | ANT | DON | COM |

| 158.2 | 380.1 | 914 | 551.6 |
| BOD | MAR | GRE | HOL |

| 617.8 | 495.6 | 640.42 | 519.5 |
| UND | MEE | YOU | AGA |

1.	2.	3.	4.	5.
6.	7.	8.	9.	10.
11.	12.	13.	14.	15.
16.	17.	18.	19.	20.

b.

551.8 BUT	591 SMI	952.01 ISH	531.6 SPU
919.5 MAC	935.01 LAN	515.1 HAE	510 NGU
519.5 MAS	994.05 BOL	574.13 VAN	994.51 EAS
512.5 IFR	591.68 HOW	915.4 JOH	513.93 ORD
914.59 PIL	510.76 BRO	573.2 LEA	949.3 HAE

1.	2.	3.	4.	5.
6.	**7.**	**8.**	**9.**	**10.**
11.	**12.**	**13.**	**14.**	**15.**
16.	**17.**	**18.**	**19.**	**20.**

c.

027.6305 MUL	338.479105 INT	363.960994 SIE	306.360941 HAN
305.235 ROS	338.064 FED	363.7384 WAL	333.33068 REA
306.30994 BRE	333.333 MAL	027.625 BRO	338.476292 JUR
027.80994 SCH	338.47910904 BUR	363.19260973 OKU	305.2350994 WHI
333.33068 CYR	306.76620994 MOD	305.230942 DES	306.380941 KIR

1.	2.	3.	4.	5.
6.	7.	8.	9.	10.
11.	12.	13.	14.	15.
16.	17.	18.	19.	20.

EXERCISE 8.3

Arrange the Dewey Decimal Classification call numbers given below in numerical order for a library collection that is totally integrated (all formats intershelved).

VIDEO 332.6324 AUS	001.64404 CHO	020.6224205 LIB	158.05 JOU
052.94 AUS	SERIAL 994.020924 WAR	333.330688 CAN	614.0994 AUS
REF 614.59623 KIL	020.941 LIB	VIDEO 641.5676 LON	333.3387 SUC
005.26 BAS	SERIAL 346.9407 BUS	001.64 STA	REF 994.03 CLU
005.262 TUR	001.6404 OGD	REF 949.5074 GAG	949.5 MEN

1.	2.	3.	4.	5.
6.	7.	8.	9.	10.
11.	12.	13.	14.	15.
16.	17.	18.	19.	20.

EXERCISE 8.4

Arrange the Dewey Decimal Classification call numbers given below in numerical order, taking note of the location symbols such as VIDEO. Arrange the numbers for a segregated collection that has the reference materials shelved at the beginning, the serials integrated with the main collection, and the videos shelved at the end.

VIDEO 509.22 DON	328.73 CON	011.38 HOP	378.33 GRA
016.35471 IND	SERIAL 590.744 INT	705.8 AME	016.31 STA
REF 791.45 CON	011.6403 NEV	VIDEO 314.2 WHI	520.321 ENG
378.43 BAR	SERIAL 021.0025 INT	021.002541 BRI	REF 001.640321 ABR
341.2 TRI	016.35494093 GAR	VIDEO 020.321 HIL	REF 328.73 AUS

1.	2.	3.	4.	5.
6.	7.	8.	9.	10.
11.	12.	13.	14.	15.
16.	17.	18.	19.	20.

EXERCISE 8.5

Arrange the Dewey Decimal Classification call numbers that include Cutter-Sanborn numbers in numerical order. Write the numbers in the boxes.

364.0994 C929	364.994021 W181	364.994021 M953	364.49 C929
363.25 L131	364 H229	346.991 W587	364.994 C297
364.099 A477	364.994 A198	364.021 D562	364.99402 C444
364 B112	364.49 M476	363.25 G255	364.49 C928
364.994021 W182	363.25 M475	360 Y92	363.25 G256

1.	2.	3.	4.	5.
6.	7.	8.	9.	10.
11.	12.	13.	14.	15.
16.	17.	18.	19.	20.

Library of Congress Classification (LCC)

LCC, which uses letters and numbers, was developed by the Library of Congress to organize its own collection. Many libraries throughout the world, particularly large academic and special libraries, have adopted it.

Subject specialists devised the LCC schedules. There are over thirty volumes in this series of special schedules, each with its own index. Letters are used to designate main classes and subclasses, and numbers are used for divisions. Gaps are left in the schedules to provide for the expansion and addition of subjects.

The main classes are:

A	General works
B	Philosophy and religion
C	History: Auxiliary sciences
D	History: General and old world
E-F	History: America
G	Geography and anthropology
H	Social sciences
J	Political science
K	Law
L	Education
M	Music
N	Fine arts
P	Language and literature
Q	Science
R	Medicine
S	Agriculture
T	Technology
U	Military science
V	Naval science
Z	Bibliography and library science

Call Numbers

Call numbers are a combination of the LC classification number plus the book number (or Cutter) plus the date. The Cutter represents the author's surname or the title and, sometimes, the geographic area. Call numbers usually include the date of publication. For example, two editions of Jenkinson's book on the chemistry of metals have the call numbers:

QD   QD
171   171
.J47   .J47
1984   1987

Procedures for Shelving a Book by Its Library of Congress Call Number

1. Begin with the first letter(s).
   e.g.,   A   AC   AG   AP   B

2. After finding the proper alphabetical section, read the numbers that follow the letters in numerical order.
   e.g.,   AP1   AP2   AP5   AP10   AP50

3. If there is a decimal point in the first row, a number to the right of the decimal point is treated as a decimal number.
   e.g.,   DS668.29   *comes before*   DS668.3

4. Books on a similar subject have call numbers that begin with the same set of letters and numbers. Each book is then identified by the remaining letter/number set in the call number. Read the letter that begins the next line of the call number in alphabetical order.
   e.g.,   AP2   AP2   AP2   AP2   AP2
           .A   .B   .D   .G   .S

5. Now read the final number group in the call number as a decimal number.
   e.g.,   AP2   AP2   AP2   AP2   AP2
           .N2   .N31   .N3545   .N4   .N489

6. When a date appears as the last line of the call number, the call numbers with the additional line follow those without the date.
   e.g.,   DS668   *comes before*   DS668
           .B39   .B39
                                         1954

7. Dates are shelved in chronological order.
   e.g.,   JV9185.I8   *comes before*   JV9185.I8
          C72   C72
          1990   1996

Example of Sequence

B	BA	BA	BA	BA	BA
1649	164	1631	1631	1631	1631
.R94	.D63	.A48	.A5	.A5	.A5
M3	N71	S55	P3	P36	P36
1964	1991	1985	1979	1978	1980

EXERCISE 8.6

List the following groups of Library of Congress Classification call numbers in order:

a.

GN	GN	GN	GN	GN
325	325	324	326	326
.F47	.F7	.F531	.F5	.F5
	1979	1986	1991	1989

1.	2.	3.	4.	5.

b.

Z699.5	Z699.5	Z699.5	Z699	Z699.5
.B53	.B53	.B5	.B53	.B53
D37	D3	D37	D3	D37
1983	1984	1985	1986	1987

1.	2.	3.	4.	5.

c.

PL2892	PL282	PL2842	PL8224	PL42
.A52	.A5	.A2	.A502	.A552
M6	M7	M61	M76	M606
1987	1942		1990	1993

1.	2.	3.	4.	5.

d.

Q1 .S34	JQ4011 .E49	BF575 .S75K44	QB1 .R47
HJ2193 .S97	TX724 .5 .B47	QB86 .S35	HJ2193 .F56
BF575 .9 .A86	QL737 .C23T475	HN850 .V5A97	QB51 .A77
HJ9931 .A44	TX717 .P43	HN850 .Z9V58	JA26 .A86
HV1 .C74	GT4985 .N38	QB1 .A89441	QB1 .5 .M67

1.	2.	3.	4.	5.
6.	7.	8.	9.	10.
11.	12.	13.	14.	15.
16.	17.	18.	19.	20.

e.

QH540 .B75	Q1 .R553	DG5 .I61	HM1 .A87
HV1 .C74	T1 .226 .U54	HM1 .A5	HN850 .Z9V53
DU967 .6 .K29	Q1 .R56	HN850 .V5A97	QH540 .C38
JA26 .A86	HQ1101 .W74	QH540 .C4	QB1 .5 .M67
QH540 .C3	HN850 .Z9V58	SD1 .7 .W4	HM1 .5 .C72

1.	2.	3.	4.	5.
6.	7.	8.	9.	10.
11.	12.	13.	14.	15.
16.	17.	18.	19.	20.

f.

HT609	QP33	QH511	RC632
.S33	.5	.H35	.P56
	.C3		I57

QP34	HD5345	QH508	QP171
.L348	.A6	.G7	.S58
	C74		

QA276	QH508	DS611	NC1115
.8	.B3	.I44	.B7
.H34			

HT609	HV9069	PA2117	HA31
.R43	.C53	.A5	.2
			.M66

HT609	JV9185	S494	R127
.R5	.I8	.5	.2
	C72	.W3	.V58

1.	2.	3.	4.	5.
6.	7.	8.	9.	10.
11.	12.	13.	14.	15.
16.	17.	18.	19.	20.

Correct Shelving Practice

To ensure users can find library materials they need, shelvers must understand how to read the classification scheme and how to file items in the correct location. Shelving is an important process in all libraries since misshelved items are lost to those who are looking for them by call number.

The materials that need to be shelved include those items that have returned from loan through the circulation desk. Other materials for shelving include:

- items that have been used in the library
- items being added to the collection
- items returned from binding and repair
- items being transferred from one part of the collection to another.

Returning materials to their correct location as quickly as possible is a priority. Efficient reshelving of materials prevents users and staff from wasting time looking for materials not on the shelf, or from speculating whether something is missing.

Busy periods often result in shelving bottlenecks and backlogs. Designated sorting areas for materials awaiting reshelving, numbered and/or dated book trucks, or special sorting shelves on different floors can assist in keeping the shelving workflow running smoothly.

Shelving Procedure

The shelving process can be divided into several steps:

1. Sort the material by format if the library does not have a fully integrated shelving system. Categories include:
     - reference books
     - fiction monographs
     - junior monographs
     - large print monographs
     - nonfiction monographs
     - videos
     - CDs
     - current periodicals
     - bound periodicals
     - microforms.

2. Sort within each format according to a broad unit—usually a range of the classification scheme. For example, sort DDC numbers by 100s, 200s, and so forth, and LCC numbers by QAs, QDs, and so on.

3. Place the items on book trucks for reshelving. Arrange the items in call number order to avoid backtracking along the shelves.

4. Shelve the items.

5. Record statistics on the number of items shelved each day.

Shelving Technique

Part of the task of shelving is to ensure that the items already on the shelves are in order and in good condition. While shelving, library staff should look out for misshelved materials and either send them for sorting or reshelve them correctly. Materials requiring repair and rebinding should be routed to the appropriate unit.

Shelves should be tidied constantly by:
- shifting all volumes to the left side of the shelf with a book support on the right to prevent leaning
- aligning volumes with spines to the front edge of the shelf
- relieving the pressure of items being packed too tightly by shifting one or two items to the shelf above or below.

To avoid damaging the books during shelving, try the following:
- making a space first with one hand rather than jamming books in
- using both hands to straighten books so that they stand upright to the left of the shelf
- carefully inserting book supports to prevent damage to the base of books.

Occupational Health and Safety (OH&S) Alert
- *Use a kick stool to work above shoulder level rather than stretching for a shelf you can barely reach.*
- *Sit on a kick stool when working below waist level rather than crouching or bending over.*
- *Pick up books with both hands rather than using one hand.*
- *Turn around using your feet rather than twisting your body.*
- *Shelve for not more than three hours a day.*
- *Try to vary tasks while shelving.*
- *Vary your movements while shelving and pay attention to your body as you move.*
- *Ensure that book trucks are evenly and not too heavily loaded because they can topple easily.*

Exercise 8.7

Some materials require different handling because of their format. Shelve examples of each of the following formats and comment on whether they were easier or harder to handle than books.

Material	Comparison with Shelving Books
Pamphlets	
Unbound serials	
Bound serials	
Microfiche	
Kits	
Videos	
Maps, charts	
Newspapers	

Revision Quiz 8.8

1. What is a closed access library?

2. Why do some libraries choose to shelve their materials in a fixed location?

3. Why do libraries use a classification scheme to organize the materials on their shelves?

4. Why is it important to reshelve items promptly?

5. Give at least three OH&S rules you should follow.

Chapter 9
DAMAGE

Introduction

A prime task for library staff is to prevent damage to the materials stored in the library. The damage may be caused by:

- incorrect handling by library users or staff
- environmental factors
- the composition of the materials.

Causes of Damage

Manual Handling

People are often described as the worst enemies of library materials because they cause so much damage intentionally and unintentionally.

- **Library users** often overuse or abuse materials, especially books: by using paper clips, pins, or staples to mark their place; by pressing on spines when photocopying; by folding over the corners of pages; by spilling food and drinks; by making pencil marks; or simply by handling materials roughly.
- **Library staff** also cause damage by carrying too many items and dropping them, by overloading book trucks, by forcing items onto tightly-packed shelves, by using inappropriate repair techniques, and so forth.
- **Library storage can be inadequate.** Each type of material needs to be considered differently, and each must be provided with its own arrangements, support, and protection.

Environment

- **Light:** Sunlight bleaches covers of books, fades colors in maps and prints, harms paper, and fades microform. Artificial light, particularly fluorescent lighting, is damaging to many library materials. On the other hand, dark surroundings encourage infestations of insects, rodents, and fungi.
- **Temperature:** Heat makes materials brittle. If materials have been stored in a cold area, condensation occurs when they are moved to warmer surroundings.
- **Humidity:** Mold and fungi grow if the air is too humid but, if the air is too dry, some library materials dry out (e.g., paper becomes brittle).
- **Atmosphere:** Sulfur dioxide in the air forms sulfuric acid that causes brittleness in paper and decomposes leather. Hydrogen sulfide, ammonia, ozone, nitrogen oxides, and aerosols may also cause damage.
- **Pests:** Insects such as silverfish and woodworms cause damage to library materials and equipment. Rats and mice eat and/or make nests in library material.
- **Composition of the materials**: Various components in library materials sometimes cause damage. For example, the acid in newsprint leads to the rapid deterioration of newspapers.

Preventing or Alleviating Damage

Manual Handling

- Libraries need to educate library users and their own staff in the correct handling methods in order to prevent overuse and abuse of the collection. It may be necessary to restrict access to more valuable or fragile materials and to substitute originals with copies.
- Library staff should be instructed in the correct techniques for repairing and covering materials.

Environment

- The library needs to monitor lighting and ensure that it is not too bright and not too dark. For example, it should control sunlight and monitor fluorescent light.
- It is important to check humidity to ensure that the air is not too dry and not too damp and to make sure that air circulates throughout the collection. The ideal environment has steady relative humidity (55%) and a steady temperature (70°F or 21°C).
- It may be necessary to fumigate the library to destroy pests. Be careful, however, that the chemicals used are not harmful to the library materials.

Composition of the Materials

- In order to prolong the life of library materials, some libraries protect them with packaging such as boxes, folders, jackets, or special storage systems.
- Library staff should clean shelves and materials regularly and ensure that materials are not packed too tightly.

Some libraries choose an alternative form of publication to preserve the intellectual content of their materials. These methods include:

- microfilming
- recording (e.g., talking books)
- entering information into a database
- scanning or digitizing.

EXERCISE 9.1

Visit a library and make comments on the following points:

The environment	
Temperature	
Light	
Cleanliness (any dust, pests?)	

The shelving	
Is it crowded?	
Are the materials in order?	
Do library staff or the users reshelve?	
Protection of materials	
What methods are used?	
Are they effective?	

Do you think this library is well maintained?

EXERCISE 9.2

Visit a library and look closely at ten monographs on a shelf. Fill in the number of monographs fitting each category.

Damage to monographs	Yes	No
Are the covers in good condition?		
Are the spines damaged?		
Is the damage at the top or base of the spines?		
Are the spines loose?		
Are there any loose pages?		
Are the corners of pages folded over?		
Are there pen or pencil marks on the pages?		
Is the text underlined or highlighted?		
Are there any torn pages?		
Is there any evidence of repair (e.g., taped spines, sticky tape)?		

EXERCISE 9.3

Choose **two** examples of non-print materials and examine them for damage. Describe the nature of the damage, explain the factors that have caused it, and suggest ways of preventing these types of damage. Write the details in the table below.

Damage to non-print materials	Example 1	Example 2
Item		
Nature of the damage		
What caused the damage?		
How could you prevent this damage?		

Library Rules

The following rules are given to users of a research library to ensure that they handle the library materials correctly.

LIBRARY RULES

Warning

This research library aims to provide its clients with the information they require to complete their research. We try to make all materials available for your use, but this depends on how our clients handle the materials. You are asked to handle materials carefully and to take note of the following rules:

1. Do not handle the books roughly.
2. Do not drop the books or leave them on the floor.
3. Do not write in the books.
4. Do not eat or drink while in the library.
5. Do not turn over or fold the pages in the books.
6. Do not lean on the books when photocopying.
7. Do not place books on top of each other.
8. Do not use pens as bookmarks.
9. Do not cut out or tear any of the pages.
10. Please return books to the book truck when you have finished.

EXERCISE 9.4

Describe how you think a client might react when given these rules. Can you suggest any improvements?

EXERCISE 9.5

Prepare a list of guidelines for a new member of the library staff on the correct handling of library materials.

Repairs

Introduction

All library staff should be on the lookout for items that need repair or rebinding. Staff notice damaged items while shelving, when materials are returned from loan, during shelf reading, and when doing an inventory. Library users may also point out damage. Repairs or rebinding should be done as soon as possible to avoid further damage. The main objective of repairing materials is to keep them available for use.

If an item is damaged, there are several options:

* repairing
* rebinding
* repackaging
* discarding if badly damaged.

Library staff complete simple repairs such as replacing spine labels, reinforcing torn or loose spines, replacing loose pages, repairing torn pages, and removing paper clips or other page markers. More difficult repairs are likely to be done by specialist staff or the items may be sent to a commercial binding firm. If the person who discovers the damage does not have the necessary skill to complete the repair, the task should be assigned to someone who can do it properly.

Simple repairs can be carried out in-house using materials purchased from library suppliers. There is a wide range of tapes that are used to mend torn pages, repair damaged spines, and attach covers or casings. Special adhesives are available for replacing loose pages or for re-attaching covers of paperbacks and spines of hardback books.

If the library staff are too busy to repair an item immediately, they should place a slip of paper in the item with a description of the damage and set it aside. They should also enter a note in the library catalog to indicate that the item will not be found on the shelf (e.g., "Item at bindery").

Repair, Rebind, or Discard?

Library staff may need to decide whether it is worthwhile to spend the time to repair an item, to send it for rebinding, or to discard it. When making this decision, the following questions should be considered:

* Is the item needed immediately by a library user?
* Does the library hold other copies of the item?
* Is it possible to purchase a replacement?
* Can the library afford to buy a replacement?
* Is the item still in demand or only used infrequently?
* How serious is the damage?
* Does the library have the equipment and supplies needed to repair the damage?
* Is the item out of date?
* Is the information available in a different format?
* Does the item belong to a special collection?
* Is the item rare or valuable?

If the decision is made to discard the item, the library catalog must be updated to record this information.

Rebinding

Collection maintenance staff need to decide whether they are able to repair an item themselves or whether they should send it to a bindery. In some cases, the cost of rebinding might be too high so the library staff will either discard the item or try to mend it themselves.

If you decide to rebind an item, you need to prepare detailed binding instructions. You should include information on the author, title, and call number as well as details on the type of binding required, style of lettering, etc. It is important to update the catalog record to let users know that the item is at the bindery and to adjust the record when the item returns to the shelves.

Binding of Serials

Many libraries prolong the life of their serial collections by binding several issues together. This ensures that the issues stay in logical order and are protected from damage.

When preparing serials for binding, library staff sort the issues into binding order, examine the issues for damage, locate missing issues, add indexes, title pages, and supplements if required, and complete an instruction sheet for the bindery.

The library maintains a binding record that includes information describing:
- which serial titles are bound
- how often a serial is bound and how many issues are in a volume
- whether the serial has a separate index that is to be included
- the form of the title and volume numbers to be printed on the spine
- the color of the binding and type of material used
- special instructions such as whether to include the advertisements.

When the serials return from the bindery, library staff check that all of the instructions have been carried out, and amend the library records to show that the serials have been bound and are back in the library. The serials are then processed and returned to the shelves.

EXERCISE 9.6

Examine a number of damaged items in different formats (e.g., monographs, serials, videos, etc.) and consider:

1.   What caused the damage?

2.   Could it be fixed in a library or does it need special treatment?

3.   Is the item worth keeping?

4.   Has past mending caused further damage?

EXERCISE 9.7

1.   Look in a library supplier's catalog and read about the products used for repair.

2.   Examine three monographs and describe what action you would take to repair each area of damage, including what material you would use. For example: "Tip in loose pages individually using a brush and adhesive."

Damage	Action
1.	
2.	
3.	

3.   Watch a video on book repair (e.g., Demco's *Protecting library materials from wear and tear*) or refer to a guide on repairing books from a library supplier (e.g., Brodart's *Book repair guide*). Complete the following repairs:
- a torn page
- a loose page
- a torn cover
- a broken spine
- a damaged or tattered spine
- a spine that has separated from the book.

4.   Examine three videos and describe what action you would take to repair each type of damage, including what material you would use. Look out for:
- damage caused by exposure to excess heat or moisture
- evidence of actual tape being handled
- damage to cassette and spools
- damage to outer case.

Damage	Action
1.	
2.	
3.	

5. Examine examples of other non-print materials and describe the damage that is likely to occur to them. Describe how you would repair these items.

Likely Damage	Action
1.	
2.	
3.	

REVISION QUIZ 9.8

1. How does a library prevent damage caused by people handling the materials?

2. Describe three features of the ideal environment for preventing damage to library materials.

3. Why is it important to repair damaged materials promptly?

4. Describe three factors that library staff need to consider when deciding whether an item is worth repairing?

5. Why do many libraries bind their serials?

Chapter 10
INVENTORY

Introduction

The inventory process enables a library to produce an accurate measure of its collection. When taking inventory of the material, the staff check for missing items by comparing a list of the library's holdings (shelf list) with:

- the material on the shelves
- records of the material on loan
- records of the material at the bindery
- other information that accounts for why material is not on the shelf at the time of the inventory.

Why Libraries Do Inventory

Major reasons libraries conduct an inventory include:

- meeting audit requirements. Libraries have a responsibility to account for property and materials and to ensure that correct financial controls apply.
- finding out how many items are missing and which areas of the collection are most affected. A library may need to improve its security arrangements if a large proportion of items are missing.
- assessing the condition of the collection and setting aside items for repair or rebinding
- preceding the implementation of a major project such as the automation of the circulation system or catalog.

Main Methods of Inventory
Complete

This is a major task for any library and is usually only done by small libraries (e.g., school libraries) or by larger libraries that are having serious problems caused by inaccurate records.

The process involves:

- recalling as many loans as possible. An amnesty may encourage users to return late items. Items urgently needed by users may be released after sighting and recording.
- shelf reading to ensure the collection is in good shelf order
- comparing items on the shelf to the shelf list and noting any missing items
- comparing missing items with binding files, the repair collection, and the list of materials held in storage
- treating the remaining items as missing and searching for them in offices, on desks, and so forth
- identifying problems such as materials with no records, duplicate copies not noted, records but no materials, and then giving the details to the cataloging section to amend the records

- withdrawing catalog records for missing items after an exhaustive search and adjusting other records to identify items as missing. Some libraries record the items as missing on the record and wait until the next inventory before removing the record, in case the item is found.

Continuous

This involves doing an inventory of one section of the library at a time. Using this method, it may take many years to complete an inventory of the whole collection.

The advantages of this approach are:

- most of the library resources are available to users
- material on short loan is not recalled
- lower concentration of staff time is required
- work in other areas of the library is not disrupted
- problems arrive in the technical services section in small batches, causing minimal disruption to other work.

A problem with this method occurs when books are shelved incorrectly, so an efficient shelf reading program must be developed.

Pilot or Sample

This involves sampling the whole collection (e.g., every 100th book). The percentage of the collection sampled depends on the accuracy of the information required—the larger the sample, the greater the accuracy.

This technique is used:

- to decide whether a full inventory is needed
- to achieve a reasonable indication of loss rate and thereby to evaluate security or purchasing policy
- to determine which areas in the library may need a full inventory.

Automated

The fastest way to conduct an inventory is to wand the barcodes on the items while they are on the shelves using a portable scanner or wand. In a manual inventory, a great deal of time is spent taking each item off the shelf and matching it against the shelf list. In an automated system, the details of the item are electronically matched and the system records the location of the item. Library staff then prepare a list of any items that are not out on loan or are not found on the shelves. These items are recorded as lost.

Many libraries do not do inventories because of the costs involved but may shelf read to ensure the collection is in order. The purpose of shelf reading is different, however, because it is intended merely to ensure that the items currently in the library are in correct order on the shelf.

Exercise 10.1

The catalog record below is for an item that is missing from a library collection. Do you think the library staff should delete the record rather than mark the item as missing? Give reasons for your decision.

You searched for the AUTHOR: simmons j	
TITLE	67 ways to protect seniors from crime / J.L. Simmons.
AUTHOR	Simmons, J.L. (Jerry Laird), 1933-
EDITION	1st Owl book ed.
PUBLISHED	New York : H. Holt, 1993.
DESCRIPT	xii, 228 p. ; 21 cm..
SUBJECT	Crime prevention -- United States.
BIBLIOG.	Includes bibliographical references.
ISBN	0805024964

	LOC'N	CALL #	STATUS
1.	Central library	362.88 SIM	Missing

Weeding

Weeding is the process of discarding library materials. The decision to weed may result from an inventory or it may be a continuous process. Weeding is often done due to a special need, particularly if a section of the library has become very crowded, leaving no room for new materials. Many libraries have developed a weeding policy that complements the selection policy and is part of the collection development policy.

Reasons for Weeding

- Information is out of date or inaccurate.
- Material is worn out physically.
- Better materials are available.
- Duplicate copies are found in the collection.
- The item has not been used or borrowed for a long time.
- Community needs and/or the curriculum has changed.
- Institutional objectives have changed, thereby changing the library's objectives.
- Unwanted material has contributed to crowded, untidy shelves that are difficult to use.
- The costs of storage are too high.

Other ways of reducing the size of the collection include:

- using compact storage or offsite storage for little-used materials
- reformatting (e.g., microfilming or digitizing to store information)
- limiting the subject areas of the collection or assigning different specializations to other libraries in a cooperative fashion.

Deciding What to Weed

Many libraries have a written weeding policy giving clear guidelines on selecting which materials to weed. Library staff examine each item to determine whether it fits the guidelines. The final decision on whether to discard an item is usually made by the professional staff who often ask for advice from clients.

When material has been removed from the open shelves, it may be stored in closed stacks, in compact shelving, or at a remote location; it may be disposed of in a sale or auction, or discarded. Some libraries prepare duplicates lists offering the unwanted items, which they distribute to other libraries. This is useful for libraries wishing to build up collections in new subject areas or trying to obtain out-of-print materials.

The final stage of weeding involves removing all records of items that have been discarded, or recording the transfer of relocated materials. The records that must be amended include the catalog, the shelf list, shelf guides, the floor plan, guides to the library, financial records, and, finally, the item itself (if it is being relocated rather than discarded).

Example of a Weeding Policy

PEARSON COLLEGE LIBRARY WEEDING GUIDELINES

The following criteria are used either separately or in combination to identify material for withdrawal. It should be stressed that they are guidelines only and are not mandatory.

Books

Age	Out-of-date or incorrect information
Use	Books not borrowed in the past three years
Relevance	Books not relevant to current curriculum both in content and learning level
Number of copies	Retain duplicates only when the item is heavily used
Physical condition	Books of antiquated appearance that may discourage use: - badly bound items - worn-out titles with dirty or missing pages or frayed binding

Titles are repaired or rebound when it is warranted by frequent use or the item's intrinsic value and when it is more costeffective than buying a replacement.

Reference

Age	Out-of-date or incorrect information
Number of copies	Retain only one copy of an item in the reference collection
Physical condition	Books of antiquated appearance that may discourage use: - badly bound items - worn-out titles with dirty or missing pages or frayed binding
Format	When material is held in more than one format, the print format may be considered for weeding
Currency	When a title is duplicated or several editions are held, only the most recent edition is housed in the reference collection

Titles are repaired or rebound when information is still current and when it is more costeffective than buying a replacement.

Audiovisual

Age	Out of date or incorrect information
Use	Material not borrowed in the past three years
Relevance	Material no longer appropriate to current curriculum both in content and learning level
Number of copies	Retain duplicates only when the item is heavily used
Physical condition	Filmstrips with torn sprockets. Audiotapes with poor sound. Videos with poor sound or visual reproduction
Format	Material in formats not compatible with available equipment

The Media Department is consulted about the costeffectiveness of repair.

Serials

Weeding in relation to serials is the process of discarding issues as a result of established serial retention policies. In this sense, weeding of serials differs from other formats because the process focuses almost solely on publication date.

Retention Policies

The following criteria may be used to develop serial retention policies:

Subject	Titles in subject areas where information is limited are retained for a minimum of five years
Indexed	Titles indexed in services held by the library are retained for a minimum of five years

Currency	Titles with information of a passing nature are retained for a maximum of one to two years
Holdings	Is the title held in another local library that allows public access? Is it available electronically?
Use	Visual observation and loan statistics

Cancellation

The following criteria are used to identify serials for cancellation. Before a serial is cancelled, and if it would be appropriate to borrow it on interlibrary loan, union lists of serials are consulted to identify other libraries holding the same title.

Relevance	Serials no longer relevant to current curriculum both in content and learning level
Use	Serials with minimal or infrequent use
Indexes	Serials not indexed
Ceased	Serials that have ceased publication and have no cumulative index
Supply	Serials with a history of erratic supply from the vendor

EXERCISE 10.2

Answer the following questions relating to the Pearson College Library weeding guidelines:

1. Do you agree with weeding all books that have not been borrowed in the last three years? Can you think of any problems associated with implementing this guideline?

2. How would library staff stay up-to-date with changes in the curriculum?

3. How would library staff decide whether a book was heavily used?

4. Why has the library decided to give preference to non-print formats of reference materials?

5. Why does the library keep only the most recent edition of reference books in the reference collection?

6. How would library staff check the physical condition of the audiovisual materials?

7. Why is the media department consulted about the cost-effectiveness of repairing audiovisual materials?

8. Why does the library check to see whether another library holds a serial before cancelling a title?

9. Why does the policy include visual observation as a measure of serial use?

REVISION QUIZ 10.3

1. Why do most libraries decide not to inventory the whole collection at once?

2. What is a shelf list?

3. Why is it important to shelf read the collection before doing an inventory?

4. Why do libraries weed their collections?

5. What types of materials are most likely to be weeded from a collection?

ANSWERS

EXERCISE 2.1

a.

Title	Once Around the Realms
Authors, editors, compilers, translators, illustrators, etc.	Brian M. Thomsen
Edition (if any)	
Place(s) of publication	201 Sheridan Springs Rd., Lake Geneva, WI 53147, U.S.A.; 120 Church End, Cherry Hinton, Cambridge CB1 3LB, U.K.
Name of publisher(s)	TSR
Date of publication	1995
Physical description	307 pages, illustrations, 18 cm. high
Series (if any)	Forgotten Realms: Fantasy Adventure
Notes (i.e., any other information you think could help to find or identify the item)	First Printing: April 1995
Numbers (ISBN, ISSN, other relevant numbers)	ISBN: 0-7869-0119-5 Library of Congress Catalog Card Number: 94-68134

b.

Title	The Storehouse of Sundry Valuables
Authors, editors, compilers, translators, illustrators, etc.	Translated by Charles Willemen
Edition (if any)	
Place(s) of publication	2620 Warring Street, Berkeley, California 94704
Name of publisher(s)	Numata Center for Buddhist Translation and Research
Date of publication	1994
Physical description	275 pages, no illustrations, 23.5 cm. high
Series (if any)	BDK English TripItaka 10-I
Notes (i.e., any other information you think could help to find or identify the item)	Bibliographical references and an index First printing, 1994 Translated from the Chinese of Kikkaya and Liu-Hsiao-piao
Numbers (ISBN, ISSN, other relevant numbers)	ISBN: 0-9625618-3-5 Library of Congress Catalog Card Number: 92-082068

c.

Title	Everything You Always Wanted to Know about Sex* *But Were Afraid to Ask
Authors, editors, compilers, translators, illustrators, etc.	Explained by David R. Reuben, M.D.
Edition (if any)	McKay edition published November 1969 Book Find Club edition published May 1970 Book-of-the-Month Club edition published June 1970 Psychology Today edition published May 1970 Bantam edition published January 1971
Place(s) of publication	Toronto, New York, London
Name of publisher(s)	Bantam Books
Date of publication	Bantam edition published January 1971
Physical description	433 pages, no illustrations, 18 cm. high
Series (if any)	
Notes (i.e., any other information you think could help to find or identify the item)	Has an index
Numbers (ISBN, ISSN, other relevant numbers)	

d.

Title	Balloons and Airships 1783-1983
Authors, editors, compilers, translators, illustrators, etc.	Lennart Ege Editor of the English edition Kenneth Munson from translation prepared by Erik Hildesheim Illustrated by Otto Frello
Edition (if any)	English edition
Place(s) of publication	London
Name of publisher(s)	Blandford Press
Date of publication	First English edition 1983
Physical description	234 pages, both color and black-and-white illustrations, 18.5 cm. high
Series (if any)	The Pocket Encyclopaedia of World Aircraft in Colour Blandford Colour Series
Notes (i.e., any other information you think could help to find or identify the item)	Different title on cover and title page Has an index
Numbers (ISBN, ISSN, other relevant numbers)	ISBN 0 7137 0568 X

EXERCISE 2.2

a.

Ben Jonson revised / Claude J. Summers and Ted-Larry Pebworth	Title and statement of responsibility
. – Rev. ed.	Edition
– New York, N.Y. : Twayne Publishers, c1999	Publication, distribution etc.
. – xix, 293 p. : port. ; 23 cm.	Physical description
– (Twayne's English authors series ; TEAS 557)	Series
Includes bibliographical references (p. 274-281) and index.	Note
ISBN 0-805-77062-3.	Standard number and terms of availability

b.

Crisis & renewal : meeting the challenge of organizational change / David K. Hurst	Title and statement of responsibility
. – Boston, Mass. : Harvard Business School Press, 1995	Publication, distribution etc.
. – xiii, 229 p. : ill. ; 25 cm.	Physical description
– (The management of innovation and change series)	Series
Includes bibliographical references (p. 198-213) and indexes.	Note
ISBN 0-875-84582-7.	Standard number and terms of availability

c.

The Cambridge illustrated history of ancient Greece / Paul Cartledge	Title and statement of responsibility
. – Cambridge, U.K. ; New York, N.Y. : Cambridge University Press, 1998	Publication, distribution etc.
. – xix, 380 p. : ill. (some col.), maps (some col.) ; 26 cm.	Physical description
– (Cambridge illustrated history)	Series
Includes bibliographical references (p. [371]-373) and index.	Note
ISBN 0-521-48196-1.	Standard number and terms of availability

d.

Psychic voyages / by the editors of Time-Life Books	Title and statement of responsibility
. – Alexandria, Va. : Time-Life Books, c1987	Publication, distribution etc.
. – 144 p. : ill. (some col.) ; 28 cm.	Physical description
– (Mysteries of the unknown)	Series
Bibliography: p. 138-140.	Note
Includes index.	Note
ISBN 0-809-46316-4.	Standard number and terms of availability

EXERCISE 2.3

a.   Hawaiian music and musicians : an illustrated history / <u>George S. Kanahele</u>.

b.   <u>Australia</u>
     : diario di un emigrante
     Publisher

c.   . – xxxiv, 406 p. : ill. ; 29 cm.
     Note

d.   Education in Canada : a bibliography = <u>L'éducation au Canada : une bibliographie</u> / E.G. Finley.
     The title in another language (French in this example).

EXERCISE 2.4

a.   O.K. you mugs : writers on movie actors / edited by Luc Sante and Melissa Holbrook Pierson. – 1st ed.
     – New York : Pantheon Books, c1999. – xvi, 284 p. : ill. ; 20 cm.
     Includes index.
     ISBN 0-37540-101-6.

b.   Exploration, conservation, preservation : a geographic perspective on natural resource use / by Susan
     L. Cutter, William H. Renwick. – 3rd ed. – New York : Wiley, c1999. – xiii, 391 p. : ill. ; 26 cm.
     Includes bibliographical references and index.
     ISBN 0-471-01810-4.

c.   The owl and the raven : an Inuit legend / written down by Lars Svensen. – Ottawa : Little Seal Books,
     1996. – 32 p. : ill. (some col.) ; 26 cm. – (Tell me a story)
     ISBN 0 48629 117 6.

d.   Sea hunters of Indonesia : fishers and weavers of Lamalera / R.H. Barnes. – Oxford : Clarendon Press,
     1996. – xvi, 467 p. : ill., maps ; 24 cm. – (Oxford studies in social and cultural anthropology)
     Simultaneously published in the USA and Canada.
     Includes bibliographical references (p. 403-430) and indexes.
     ISBN 0 198 28070 X (hardback). – ISBN 0 198 28072 6 (pbk.)

EXERCISE 2.5

a.   Schaum's outline of theory and problems of intermediate algebra / Ray Steege. – New York :
     McGraw-Hill, c1997. – 381 p. : ill. ; 28 cm.
     Includes index.
     ISBN 0-07060-839-3 (pbk.)

b.   Chicken soup for the soul at work : 101 stories of courage, compassion, and creativity in the
     workplace / Jack Canfield ... [et al.]. – Deerfield Beach, Fla. : Health Communications, c1996. – xvi,
     330 p. : ill. ; 22 cm.
     Includes bibliographical references.
     ISBN 1-55874-424-X.

c.   The discovery of the Titanic / by Robert D. Ballard ; with Rick Archbold ; introduction by Walter
     Lord ; illustrations of the Titanic by Ken Marschall. – New York, N.Y. : Warner Books, 1987. – 230 p.
     : ill. (some col.) ; 29 cm.
     "A Warner/Madison Press Book."
     Includes index.
     ISBN 0-44651-385-7.

d.   It's here— somewhere! / Alice Fulton and Pauline Hatch ; illustrations by Shunichi Yamamoto. – 1st ed. – Cincinnati, Ohio : Writer's Digest Books, c1985. – 179 p. : ill. ; 23 cm.
Bibliography: p. [174]-175.
Includes index.
ISBN 0-89879-186-3 (pbk).

EXERCISE 2.6

a.

Esteticheskaia vyrazitelnost goroda	title proper
otvetstvennyi redaktor O. A. Shvidkovskii	statement of responsibility
Moskva	place of publication
Nauka	publisher
1986	date of publication
156 p. : ill. ; 22 cm.	physical description
At head of title: Akademiia nauk SSSR.	note
Includes bibliographical references.	note

b.

Mellan byrakrati och laissez faire	title proper
en studie av Camillo Sittes och Patrick Geddes stadsplaneringsstrategier	other title information
Lilian Andersson	statement of responsibility
Goteborg, Sweden	place of publication
Acta Universitatis Gothoburgensis	publisher
c1989	copyright date
337 p. : ill. ; 25 cm.	physical description
(Gothenburg studies in the history of science and ideas ; 9)	series statement **OR** series title and number in series
Summary in English.	note
Thesis (doctoral)--Goteborgs universitet, 1989.	note
Includes bibliographical references (p. 321-334).	note
ISBN 9 17346 204 7.	standard number **OR** ISBN

EXERCISE 2.7

a.   Map: from the GMD. Scale 1:250,000. Dimensions (size)

b.   Videorecording: from the GMD. Other physical details (sound, color). A summary note

c.   Periodical: the chronological designation and an open date of publication. The first issue numbered "Volume 1" was published in the summer of 1966. ISSN (International Standard Serial Number)

d.   Sheet music: from the GMD. That it is music for both voice and piano. Date of publication.

e.   Electronic book (e-book): from the GMD and from the name of the publisher (netLibrary). It was published in paper format in 1998. Other title information.

EXERCISE 3.1

2.   A library might keep a later edition or differently bound edition of an item as long as a particular edition was not specifically ordered.

EXERCISE 3.2

2.   Electronic journal subscriptions are new, and the policies and procedures for them are still evolving. They are accessed over networks, so they are not shipped to the library and checked in. Usernames, passwords, and links to remote websites must be maintained. Because holdings information is a challenge to keep updated, library catalogs often do not indicate what issues are available.

REVISION QUIZ 3.3

1.   Faxed forms, email messages, forms in the mail, electronic requests via OCLC or regional networks.

2.   Rare, fragile items; material in the reference collection; periodicals are often not loaned because if they go missing it will ruin the set and they are very difficult to replace.

3.   Local courier; certified mail; overnight courier.

4.   Libraries are allowed to copy material for another library if:
      - the copy will be used for research or teaching, not for business
      - the copy includes a notice of copyright.
      Copies made for use in the classroom are also permitted.

EXERCISE 4.1

Standard access points include:
- author, added authors and other contributors, corporate bodies
- title, series title
- subjects

Many OPACs allow searches by call number and ISBN/ISSN.

EXERCISE 4.2
a. i. Pound, Roscoe, 1870-1964
    ii. No.

b. i. Yes.
    ii. Yes.

EXERCISE 4.3
a. i.   All headings are valid.
    ii. The client will be informed of the other headings possible for this author.
    iii. Yes, this author has written under a number of pseudonyms.

b. i.   United States. Immigration and Naturalization Service
    ii. Related term
    iii. Yes, if the library has works published under all names.

EXERCISE 4.4
a. i.   Book/monograph
    ii. Hell's cartographers : some personal histories of science fiction writers
    iii. Alfred Bester, and others
    iv. Yes, it has portraits.
    v.   0060100524
    vi. It is a collective biography of American science fiction writers.

b. i.   Map
    ii. Arches National Park, Utah
    iii. Colored
    iv. A firm called Trails Illustrated
    v.   Hiking trails in the Arches National Park in Utah

EXERCISE 4.5
a. i.   Monograph
    ii.   Nicholas Cox
    iii. Freeman Collins for Nicholas Cox
    iv.   1686
    v.   3rd ed.
    vi.   Yes
    vii. No
    viii. Fowling, Hunting, Falconry, Fishing, Forestry law and legislation—Great Britain, Game-laws—Great Britain
    ix.   Look up the subjects in the catalog. You may be able to navigate directly from the subject headings.
    x.   Dewey Decimal Classification
    xi.   It may be rare or fragile (it is very old).

b. i.   Videorecording
    ii.   John Heminway
    iii. WNET, New York and BBC
    iv.   Brain—Aging, Aging, Aged—Diseases, Brain—Diseases
    v.   56 min.

c. i.   Periodical
    ii.   1969
    iii.   English, French or Spanish
    iv.   Look up the subjects in the catalog. You may be able to navigate directly from the subject headings in a web-based catalog by clicking on the subject headings.

EXERCISE 4.7

a. i.   Yes - look for periodical title
    ii.   Yes - look under title
    iii.   No - individual journal articles are not usually listed in the catalog
    iv.   Yes - look under subject
    v.   No - individual journal articles are not usually listed in the catalog

b. OPACs do not all function in the same way, but here are some common approaches:
    i.   choose journals and newspapers from the main menu or
           search for author, title, etc., and limit by periodicals/magazines
    ii.   choose music/oral histories from the main menu or
           search for author, title, etc., and limit by sound recording
    iii.   search for author, title, etc., and look for [microform] after the title proper
    iv.   search for author, title, etc., and look for [electronic resource] after the title proper or
           search for author, title, etc., and limit by computer software
    v.   search for author, title, etc., and look in the physical description for monographs with fewer than 50 pages

c. Your library may use different names. Here are some common headings:
    i.   Alcott, Louisa May, 1832-1888
    ii.   United States. Internal Revenue Service
    iii.   Galleria nazionale d'arte moderna (Italy)
    iv.   American Enterprise Institute for Public Policy Research
    v.   National Baseball Hall of Fame and Museum

d. Your library may use different subject headings. Here are some common headings:
    i.   Computer software—Testing
    ii.   Football
    iii.   Stamp collecting—Periodicals
    iv.   School children—Mental health
           School children—Mental health services
           Teenagers—Mental health
           Teenagers—Mental health services
           Youth—Mental health
           Youth—Mental health services
           Child mental health services
           Mental health
    v.   Economic assistance—Developing countries
           Grants-in-aid—Developing countries

EXERCISE 4.9

a.   Air and space resources
     Air conditioning
     Air cushion vehicles
     Air Force
     Air, Lesley
     Air pollution
     Air transport
     Aircraft
     Airfields
     Airports

b.   Engineers unlimited
     Engines and trains
     England and the near east
     Englisch Sprechen!
     Englische dogges
     English historical documents
     English literature
     English men of literature
     Englishmen
     The enigma of drug addiction

c.   Go down Moses
     Go tell it on the mountain
     Goannas
     Gold and silver
     Gold fever
     Gold mining
     Golden girls
     Golf for amateurs
     Gondolas of Venose
     Gone is gone
     Good housekeeping
     Good wives
     Goodbye cruel world
     Goodness gracious me
     Goody Townhouse

d.   Booby
     Book
     Book lice
     Book of common order
     Book of common prayer
     Book of English essays
     Book of famous ships
     Book of the dead
     Book scorpion
     Book worm
     Bookbinding
     Bookish
     Bookplate
     Books
     Books and reading

Books that count
Booksellers and bookselling
Boole, George

e.   A is for alphabet
     The Acts
     An Approach to Hamlet
     Approach to housing
     An April After
     Archaeology and Old Testament
     The Archaeology of Carajou
     The Danger of Equality
     Danger on the ski trails
     La la
     Label manufacturing
     Le laboratoire
     The labour gang
     The labrador puppies
     Ladders and snakes
     Le Lagon
     La laine
     The language laboratory
     The laundry basket
     Lexicon of jargon
     A Lexicon of the German language
     That was summer
     That's me
     That's the way

f.   12 x 8 : Paper read to the Crown Club
     $12 to May
     20 + 20 = 40
     20/- change
     20% profit
     Twelve angry jelly beans
     Twelve drunk teddy bears
     Twenty and two
     Twenty poems
     Twenty soldiers

g.   4 favorite epic poems
     14 = 10 + 4
     $14 a day to tour Europe
     14 days of Hell in the Pacific
     14 lbs.
     14% of a lifetime
     44 favorite short poems
     Four and forty
     Fourteen equates to ...?
     Fourteen likely lads

EXERCISE 4.10

a.   Air and space resources
Air conditioning
Aircraft
Air cushion vehicles
Airfields
Air Force
Air, Lesley
Air pollution
Airports
Air transport

b.   Engineers unlimited
Engines and trains
England and the near east
Englische dogges
Englisch Sprechen!
English historical documents
English literature
Englishmen
English men of literature
Enigma of drug addiction

c.   Goannas
Go down Moses
Gold and silver
Golden girls
Gold fever
Gold mining
Golf for amateurs
Gondolas of Venose
Gone is gone
Goodbye cruel world
Good housekeeping
Goodness gracious me
Good wives
Goody Townhouse
Go tell it on the mountain

d.   Booby
Book
Bookbinding
Bookish
Book lice
Book of common order
Book of common prayer
Book of English essays
Book of famous ships
Book of the dead
Bookplate
Books
Books and reading
Book scorpion
Booksellers and bookselling

Books that count
Book worm
Boole, George

EXERCISE 4.11

a.   The order is letter by letter.
       The terms with the first word "Cape" are not all filed together.
       The space between Cape and Preston is ignored.

b.   The order is word by word.
       The terms with the first word "File" are all filed together.

c.   The order is word by word.
       CD-ROM viewing comes before CD-ROMs.
       Free form comes before FreeCell.

d.   The order is letter by letter.
       Spaces are ignored.
       Hawkesbury comes before Hawkes Butchery.

EXERCISE 4.12

a.   There will be some explanation found immediately before the main alphabetical listing of names.

b.   Numbers: as if they are spelled out
       Mc and Mac: as if spelled "Mac"
       Mt and Mount: as if spelled "Mount"
       St and Saint: as if spelled "Saint"
       Businesses using people's names: look under first name; check under both names
       Businesses starting with "The": usually ignore "The"; check in both places
       Punctuation and special characters: ignore
       Initials: treat as a name, regardless of punctuation
       Prefixes of names: treated as part of the first word
       Hyphenated names: treated as two words and filed under the first name

EXERCISE 4.13

a.   *An encyclopedia of rock*. Washington, DC: Schirmer, 1987.

       Manuel, Peter. *Popular music of the non-Western world: an introductory survey.* Oxford: OUP, 1988.

       Manuella, Timothy W. *Rock around the Bloc: a history of rock music in Eastern Europe and the Soviet Union.* Oxford: OUP, 1990.

       The music and the musicians: pickers, slickers, cheatin' hearts, and superstars. Chicago: Abbeville, 1988.

       Rees, Dafydd and Crampton, Luke. *Rock movers and shakers.* Cardiff: ABC-CLIO, 1991.

       Rees, David and Markoff, John. "Led Zeppelin" in *Music and musicians*, No. 54, September 1994, p. 2-7.

Robertson, Fred. *Lissauer's Encyclopedia of popular music in America, 1800 to the present*. New York: Paragon, 1991.

Robinson, D. C., *Music at the margins: popular music and global cultural diversity*. Edinburgh: Sage, 1991.

Saint, John, *The Penguin encyclopedia of popular music*. London: Viking, 1989.

St John, A. J. "I knew Elvis", *Canberra times*, 21 November 1959, p. 6.

Stumbler, Irwin. *The encyclopedia of pop, rock and soul*. Chicago: St. Martin's Country Music Foundation, 1989.

b.   *An accent on periodicals: a survey*. Canberra: Library Association of Australia, 1989.

Access: the supplementary index to Internet serials. Washington, DC: Gaylord, 1975-

I.B.M. journal of research and development. New York: International Business Machines Corporation, 37, 1993.

I.T. and accounting: the impact of information technology, edited by Bernard C. Williams and Barry J. Spaul. London: Chapman & Hall, 1991.

I.T.: journal of information technology. Sydney, Australia: Macquarie University, 1995-

IEEE/ACM transactions on networking. New York: Institute of Electrical and Electronics Engineers and the Association for Computing Machinery, 2:2, Winter 1994.

IEEE annals of the history of computing. Los Alamitos, Calif.: IEEE Computer Society, 1979-

IEEE transactions on communications. New York: Institute of Electrical and Electronics Engineers, 15:8, August 1995.

IEEE transactions on computers. New York: Institute of Electrical and Electronics Engineers, 1959-

IEEE transactions on information technology. New York: Institute of Engineers, 1955-

Information sources in information technology, editor, David Haynes. London: Bowker-Saur, 1990.

Information technology and libraries. Chicago: American Library Association, 17:3, March 1998.

NATO Advanced Study Institute on Information Technology and the Computer Network. *Information technology and the computer network*, edited by Kenneth G. Beauchamp. Berlin: Springer-Verlag, 1984.

EXERCISE 4.14

3rd world report
4 weekly poets
24 hours: ABC FM program
Abridged reader's guide to periodical literature
Book review digest
Booklist
The bulletin
Bulletin of the Centre for Children's Books
C.S.R. quarterly report
CSIRO papers
Defence index
Defense abstracts
Four to fourteen
The horn book magazine
A journal of documentation
The journal of early childhood behavior
Mount Morgan mining review
Mt Isa Mines ecological quarterly
Queensland agricultural review
Queensland. Dept of Education. Annual report
Social science abstracts
Sociofile

EXERCISE 4.15

20th Century Britain
100 ideas for the pianist
106 funny things
114 ways to be your own boss
150 masterpieces of drawing
160 feet down
1050 jewellery designs
1200 Chinese basic characters
1200 notes, quotes, and anecdotes
1250 years at Westbury
150,000 years
160,000 kilowatts
Oliver, I. J.
Oliver Pty Ltd
Olivers galore
One Australia
One hundred and two H bombs
One single minute
One thing necessary
One thousand and one fishing trips
One thousand and one nights
One two buckle my shoe
O'Neill, Fred J.
O'Neil's private war
T. W. U. report
TV Shopping Network
Twelve lesson course
Twelve noon

The twentieth century
Twentieth century drama

EXERCISE 4.16

The filing principles are:
- numbers are filed as if spelled out
- initial articles are ignored.

One Australia
150 masterpieces of drawing
150,000 years
114 ways to be your own boss
106 funny things
160 feet down
113 teams of netball players
112 2nd form students
One hundred and two H bombs
100 ideas for the pianist
100,000 jelly beans in a bag
One single minute
1050 jewelry designs
1001 fishing trips
One thousand and one nights
One two buckle my shoe
30 bald heads
'39 to '94: the years of change
3000 elephants in a Mini?
3111 buttons
3001 days to blast off
3001: the year of the future
3010 pieces of paper
3101 feet of rope
Twelve lesson course
12 noon
The twentieth century
20th century Britain
Twentieth century drama

EXERCISE 5.1

1. City planning—Research. Architecture, Environmental aspects—Research. Design—Research.
    Sage Publications for the College of Environmental Design, University of California, Berkeley.
    No, it ceased in 1971.

2. The following are criticisms of Margaret Atwood's *The handmaid's tale*:
    Wilson, Sharon Rose, et al., *Approaches to teaching Atwood's* The handmaid's tale and other works
    Foster, Malcolm, *Margaret Atwood's* The handmaid's tale
    Michael, Magali Cornier, *Feminism and the postmodern impulse: post-World War II fiction*
    Thompson, Lee Briscoe, *Scarlet letters: Margaret Atwood's* The handmaid's tale

3. Critical companions to popular contemporary writers

4.   For the birds : a book about air / by Jill Wheeler ; illustrated by Angela Kamstra and Krista Schaeppi.

5.   STACS 2000 : 17th Annual Symposium on Theoretical Aspects of Computer Science, Lille, France, February 17-19, 2000 : proceedings

6.   John Lennon, 1940-1980

7.   *Los aztecas : poesías tomados de los antiguos contares mexicanos.* Published by Factoria Ediciones. Originally published in 1854.

8.   *Cloudy with a chance of meatballs* [braille] by Judi Barrett. Published by National Braille Press.

9.   There are many books by Neil Simon, including the following:
        Barefoot in the park
        Biloxi blues
        Brighton Beach memoirs
        California suite
        The goodbye girl
        The odd couple

10.   There are also a number of books about Neil Simon, including the following:
        Johnson, Robert K., *Neil Simon*
        Konas, Gary, *Neil Simon: a casebook*
        McGovern, Edythe M., *Neil Simon, a critical study*
        McGovern, Edythe M., *Not-so-simple Neil Simon: a critical study*
        Simon, Neil, *The play goes on: a memoir*

EXERCISE 5.2

OCLC Symbol	NUC Symbol	Library
DY3	NmTr	Truth or Consequences Public Library
NJF	NcGCL	Center for Creative Leadership Library
SSK	FKeNKS	NASA, John F. Kennedy Space Center
GPG	CtMyMHi	Mystic Seaport Museum, G.W. Blunt White Library
IUF	TxDaM-L	Southern Methodist University, Underwood Law
BIA	ViQF	Federal Bureau of Investigation, Academy Library

EXERCISE 5.3

1.   Marcel Desaulniers' *Death by chocolate cakes* is held by many libraries, including:
        DLC   Library of Congress
        MLN   Minuteman Library Network
        NTG   King County Library System
        UOK   Seattle Public Library

2.   Barbara Kingsolver's *The poisonwood bible* is held by many libraries, including:

    ANQ   Notre Dame Academy
    NPL   Free Public Library of Newark, New Jersey
    ZTP   Boces, Onondaga, Cortland & Madison
    BEL   US Army, Van Noy Library

3.   *The complete climber's handbook* is held by many libraries, including:

    YCC   Yuma County Library District
    CVL   Chula Vista Public Library
    BIB   Bibliomation, Inc.
    IUL   Indiana University
    OCP   Public Library of Cincinnati/Hamilton County

4.   *A community checklist : important steps to end violence against women : "—what can we do about it?"* is held by many libraries, including:

    AKD   Central Arkansas Library System
    DLA   Widener University School of Law, Delaware Campus
    IWN   North Iowa Area Community College
    XLJ   Montgomery County Department of Public Libraries
    MTS   State Law Library of Montana
    VVJ   John Jay College of Criminal Justice Library
    BHS   Black Hills State University
    VTT   Vermont Law School

5.   *The Georgia plant list : a list of the Georgia plants in the University of Georgia Herbarium* is held by:

    DBD   Denver Botanic Gardens-Helen Fowler Library
    COQ   Southeast Metropolitan Board of Cooperative Services
    MOA   Missouri Botanical Garden

EXERCISE 5.4

a.   Women & literature : a journal of women writers and the literary treatment of women

    CTW   Eastern Connecticut State University Library
    UCW   University of Connecticut Library
    WLU   Wesleyan University Library
    YUS   Yale University Library

b.   1996. http://www.jsi.com/intl/omni/pubs.htm

c.   January 1907

d.   International journal of purchasing and materials management (ISSN 1055-6001); Journal of purchasing and materials management (ISSN 0094-8594); Journal of purchasing (ISSN 0022-4030)

e.   Montana Technical Library (MZJ). Most recent title is Occupational health & safety.

f.   University of Michigan. Worm runners digest

g.   Yes. Wilson County Public Library (UZJ) and John A. Stahl Library (NWD)

h.   177. Includes university, college, school, government, medical, and public

i.   Yes to both questions.

j.   Ceased in 1998 but is continued by ALCTS newsletter online. Pepperdine University notes that it is permanently retaining the complete holdings.

EXERCISE 5.5

a.   Yes. It is a serial, published biennially.

b.   Achterhuis. 1995.

c.   American birds / National Audubon Society. Yes, it has changed its name twice:
Earlier title: Audubon field notes (ISSN 0097-7144)
Later title: National Audubon Society field notes (ISSN 1078-5477)

d.   Draft general management plan, environmental impact statement Death Valley National Park, Inyo and San Bernardino Counties, California, Nye and Esmeralda Counties, Nevada.

e.   There are four catalogs in the Library of Congress about collecting Beanie Babies in the United States published in 1998:
Beanie family album and collector's guide / by Shawn Brecka.
Beanie tracker : an inventory book and buyer's guide to The Beanie Babies / by R. A. Downey.
Encyclo-beanie-a : ultimate guide / Tiffany Foucht, Rachel Cook, Dawna Foucht.
Beanie babies : collector's guide / Holly Stowe.

f.   Information brokers and reference services (1988)
Conflicts in reference services
International aspects of reference and information services
Reference services and public policy
The reference library user : problems and solutions
Opportunities for reference services : the bright side of reference services in the 1990's
Reference service expertise
Reference services and education
Information brokers and reference services (1989)
The publishing and review of reference sources
Reference services today : from interview to burnout

g.   Farmers' and farm workers' movements : social protest in American agriculture / Patrick H. Mooney and Theo J. Majka.
Conquering Goliath : Cesar Chavez at the beginning / Fred Ross ; foreword by Edward M. Kennedy.
Jessie De La Cruz : profile of a United Farm worker / Gary Soto.

h.   5th ed. 1999. Z696 .U4 C47 1999.

i.   Hachette Filipacchi USA, Inc. Oct./Nov. 1995.

j.   Coupland, Douglas, Generation X : tales for an accelerated culture.

	Books	Periodicals	Non-Book Materials
Print	Books in Print Whitaker's Books in Print Forthcoming Books International Books in Print Livres disponibles = French books in print	Ulrich's International Periodicals Directory	Guide to Microforms in Print Words on Cassette The Software Encyclopedia Bowker's Complete Video Directory CD-ROMs in Print The Multimedia and CD-ROM Directory
CD-ROM	Books in Print plus Books Out of Print plus Global Books in Print on Disc SciTech Reference plus Libros en venta plus = Spanish books in print plus	Ulrich's plus SciTech Reference plus	The Multimedia and CD-ROM Directory CD-ROMs in Print Bowker's Complete Video Directory A-V Online
Online	Books in Print Online http://www.globalbooksinprint.com	Ulrichsweb.com	Microcomputer Software Guide Online A-V Online

EXERCISE 5.11

b.   Midwest Library Service: www.midwestls.com
       Blackwells: www.blackwell.com
       Yankee Book Peddlar: www.ybp.com
       Elsevier Science: www.elsevier.com
       Addison Wesley Longman: www.awlonline.com
       Borders: www.borders.com

d.   i.   Thomas Evan.

       ii.   There are many books by Daniel Boorstin, including:
               Cleopatra's nose : essays on the unexpected.
               The creators : a history of heroes of the imagination.
               The birth of the Republic, 1763-1789.
               The discoverers.
               The seekers : the story of man's continuing quest to understand his world.

       iii.   Prices vary. Yes, it is available in audiocassette.

       iv.   12 of Patricia Cornwell's novels are available.
               All that remains; Black notice; Body farm; Body of evidence; Cause of death; Cruel and
               unusual; From Potter's Field; Hornets nest; Point of origin; Postmortem; Southern cross;
               Unnatural exposure.

       v.   Random House.

       vi.   Yes.

       vii.   Flight 111 : the tragedy of the Swissair crash / Stephen Kimber.
               ISBN: 0770428401.

       viii.   Librarian's handbook
               Periodicals for business
               Electronic media catalog
               Periodicals for law libraries
               Periodicals for schools
               Periodicals for the health services
               Periodicals for public libraries, and
               Ebsco bulletin of serial changes, to which libraries need to subscribe.

EXERCISE 5.12

Sources are not specified because the answers can usually be found in more than one.

1.   i.   Ernest E. Fitzgerald. 1998
       ii.   Mystery and detective fiction. Yes: Time to be in earnest: a fragment of autobiography
       iii.   The Nancy Drew notebooks
       iv.   rcottom@mdhs.org. http://www.mdhs.org
       v.   Warner Books (hardback); Wheeler (large type); Time Warner (audiocassette)
       vi.   0736804749
       vii.   Robert Boyd. How humans evolved. 2nd edition
       viii.   Stories subversive: through the field with gloves off
               Purple springs
               In times like these

  ix. 3320 Alderwood Ave., Bellingham WA 98225-1102; 360-734-1908
  x. Canadian Library Association

2. i. Robert Starer. H. Leonard. 0793542022
  ii. Statistics for life sciences. 2nd ed.
  iii. Yes. 7/16 Ansari Road, Daryaganj, New Delhi 110 002, India
  iv. Login Brothers. 800-665-1148; www.lb.com
  v. Yes. 1994

3. i. Yes. Peace and East-West relations (out of print)
  ii. Ethical & religious thought in analytic philosophy of language
  iii. Sir Gawain & the Green Knight: a dual language edition
    Pearl: an edition with verse translation
  iv. William-Alan Landes
  v. Pierre Trudeau. Yes. $45 U.S.
  vi. 0811820114
  vii. Read my lips, make my day, eat quiche, and die!
  viii. 4th ed.
  ix. 33 W. Grand Ave., Suite 301, Chicago IL 60610-4306; Phone: 312-644-1896; Fax: 312-644-1899; ila@ila.org
  x. Challenge to Mars: pacifism from 1918 to 1946

4. i. www.photodisc.com Animal patterns; ClipPix; Ethereal shadows
  ii. Cloud 9 Interactive. $34.95 U.S. Elementary and secondary school. Yes
  iii. There are lots of titles. You may need to limit your search.

5. i. Quakezone (1993)
    Spinning things; earthquakes (1996)
    Killer quake! (1994)
  ii. 2000 Duke St., Alexandria VA 22314. Phone: 703-838-7493. Fax: 703-838-6915

6. i. 1984. 3 times per year
  ii. Yes. Print and CD-ROM
  iii. Bob Gibbons, Syracuse NY. Bimonthly
  iv. McLean County Independent. 3,875 (paid)
  v. 0022-166X. $54 to individuals; $113 to institutions
  vi. December 1996. Yes
  vii. Electric perspectives. Edison Electric Institute, Washington D.C.

EXERCISE 5.13

Name	Entry Element
Liu Yen	Liu, Yen
Defense Dept.	Depends on whose Defense Department it is; e.g., Australia, United States, Canada
Vijay Joshi	Joshi, Vijay
Chi Do Pham	Pham, Chi Do
Hung Sheng	There are many people with this name—more information is needed
United States Geological Survey	Geological Survey (U.S.)
Fletcher Jones Pty Ltd	Fletcher Jones and Staff Pty Ltd

Oreste Vaccari	Vaccari, Oreste
Desh Gupta	Gupta, Desh
Ray Charles	Charles, Ray, 1930-
Prince Charles	Charles, Prince of Wales, 1948-
Charles II	Charles II, King of England, 1630-1685
Sommai Premchit	Sommai Premchit
Jalal al Ahmad	al Ahmad, Jalal
Omar Khayyam	Omar Khayyam

EXERCISE 5.14

i.   Weiers, Pamela S., and Jill Safro, Birnbaum's Walt Disney World without kids 1999, Hyperion and Hearst, ISBN: 0786883707, $11.95 (U.S.).
ii. Ambrose, James E., and Harry Parker, Simplified design of concrete structures, 7th ed., J. Wiley & Sons, ISBN: 0471139181, $80.00 (U.S.).
iii. Go, Frank M., Tom Baum, and Mary Monachello, Human resource management in the hospitality industry, J. Wiley & Sons. ISBN: 0471110566, $64.95 (U.S.).
iv. Ecuador and the Galapagos Islands, $19.99 (U.S.).
v.   National Vital Statistics Report, National Center for Health Statistics (U.S.), 1999-

EXERCISE 6.1

Answers might include:

Type of Library	Client Group
Public library	General public living or working in a particular local government area including: children, adults, senior citizens, and special groups such as housebound, physically disabled, visually impaired Public from out of the area upon payment of a deposit or fee
School or academic library	Teaching staff, administrative staff, students, parents, occasionally staff from similar institutions Public upon payment of a deposit or fee
National library	Staff, other libraries, scholars and researchers, and the public
Special library	Employees (may be divided into different categories of employees) Employees from related or cooperating organizations, contractors upon payment of a fee or deposit

Exercise 6.3
Answers might include:

Type of Library	Proof of Identification
School library	Students: name on class list, student card Teachers: pay slip, name on staff list
Academic library	Students: student card, instructor's letter, fee receipt Staff: pay slip or staff identification card Staff from similar institutions: pay slip, letter of introduction
Special library	Security identification, pay slip, supervisor's authority

Revision Quiz 6.8
1. In order to provide different services for different clients according to their needs.
2. When there is a need to keep a client's signature showing agreement to the conditions of borrowing material.
3. b
4. The circulation desk is usually the most frequent point of contact for library clients. Clients may judge all library services on the quality of service they receive at the circulation desk.
5. The slip is used to show when items are due back in the library. Its use saves staff time stamping the due date on each of the items being borrowed.
6. To make it possible to introduce self-checkout stations into the library.
7. When they require the item for a longer period.
8. Fines are imposed to encourage clients to return library materials by the due date. This helps to make the materials available for other library clients to use.

Exercise 6.9
Issues for library staff include:
- extra space to keep the materials in a secure area and prevent unauthorized use
- extra staffing to retrieve materials for students and to book items
- extra marking of items to identify their status more easily
- rudeness and distress of clients who are unable to access an item when needed, especially just before assignments are due
- communication with teachers so that material is put into the reserve collection when students need it
- ensuring that teachers review the collection regularly so that only required material is kept on reserve
- students might rely only on material put aside for them rather than using the whole collection.

Issues for clients include:
- heavy fines and penalties discouraging use
- high demand for some materials and limited loan periods restricting use
- an in-library-only use policy disadvantaging part-time and distance education students
- the need to plan ahead rather than waiting until deadlines are imminent

Revision Quiz 6.10

1. A large number of clients need access to a restricted number of items, usually for a short time.
2. - shorter loan periods of a few hours or overnight
   - often housed in a secure area of library and often only for use in the library
   - heavy fines and penalties if not returned on time
   - can be reserved/booked for a particular time
3. - the library's collection
   - teachers' personal copies
   - lecture notes, tapes
   - photocopies temporarily made available
4. - most academic libraries
   - some school libraries
   - some special libraries

Revision Quiz 7.9

1. It is important to maintain a library's collection because:
   - Library materials are often expensive or impossible to replace
   - Materials should be kept in good condition and order to make sure that they are accessible and ready to use
   - Users are more inclined to use materials that are in good condition and tend to avoid shabby or damaged material.

2. A spine label is a label that is stuck on the spine of library materials to show the call number and location details for an item.

3. Libraries cover books to strengthen them and to protect them from damage and soiling.

4. Final processing is the physical preparation of library materials for inclusion in the collection. It may involve covering or strengthening them or protecting them by placement in boxes or folders.

5. Factors that affect the storage methods chosen by a library include:
   - cost
   - appearance
   - the space available
   - the library's clientele
   - the need to prevent damage to materials
   - staffing levels
   - the rarity of the materials
   - the special needs of specific formats.

Exercise 8.1

1. F/ARC	2. F/GRI	3. F/KOC (Highways)	4. F/KOC (Year)	5. F/MCC
6. F/RUS	7. F/THE (Happy)	8. F/THE (My other)	9. F/TRO (Men)	10. F/TRO (Next)

EXERCISE 8.2

a.

1.	2.	3.	4.	5.
004.1 COM	025.1 ORG	158.2 BOD	302.2 COM	331.12 LIF
6.	7.	8.	9.	10.
380.1 MAR	428 FRO	495.6 MEE	519.5 AGA	551.6 HOL
11.	12.	13.	14.	15.
617.8 UND	640.42 YOU	796.46 ATL	808.02 ESS	822.3 CRE
16.	17.	18.	19.	20.
882.01 ANT	914 GRE	940.28 IND	944 LAN	959.86 DON

b.

1.	2.	3.	4.	5.
510 NGU	510.76 BRO	512.5 IFR	513.93 ORD	515.1 HAE
6.	7.	8.	9.	10.
519.5 MAS	531.6 SPU	551.8 BUT	573.2 LEA	574.13 VAN
11.	12.	13.	14.	15.
591 SMI	591.68 HOW	914.59 PIL	915.4 JOH	919.5 MAC
16.	17.	18.	19.	20.
935.01 LAN	949.3 HAE	952.01 ISH	994.05 BOL	994.51 EAS

c.

1.	2.	3.	4.	5.
027.625 BRO	027.6305 MUL	027.80994 SCH	305.230942 DES	305.235 ROS
6.	7.	8.	9.	10.
305.2350994 WHI	306.30994 BRE	306.360941 HAN	306.380941 KIR	306.76620994 MOD
11.	12.	13.	14.	15.
333.33068 CYR	333.33068 REA	333.333 MAL	338.064 FED	338.476292 JUR
16.	17.	18.	19.	20.
338.479105 INT	338.47910904 BUR	363.19260973 OKU	363.7384 WAL	363.960994 SIE

EXERCISE 8.3

1. 001.64 STA	2. 001.6404 OGD	3. 001.64404 CHO	4. 005.26 BAS	5. 005.262 TUR
6. 020.6224205 LIB	7. 020.941 LIB	8. 052.94 AUS	9. 158.05 JOU	10. VIDEO 332.6324 AUS
11. 333.330688 CAN	12. 333.3387 SUC	13. SERIAL 346.9407 BUS	14. 614.0994 AUS	15. REF 614.59623 KIL
16. VIDEO 641.5676 LON	17. 949.5 MEN	18. REF 949.5074 GAG	19. SERIAL 994.020924 WAR	20. REF 994.03 CLU

EXERCISE 8.4

1. REF 001.640321 ABR	2. REF 328.73 AUS	3. REF 791.45 CON	4. 011.38 HOP	5. 011.6403 NEV
6. 016.31 STA	7. 016.35471 IND	8. 016.35494093 GAR	9. SERIAL 021.0025 INT	10. 021.002541 BRI
11. 328.73 CON	12. 341.2 TRI	13. 378.33 GRA	14. 378.43 BAR	15. 520.321 ENG
16. SERIAL 590.744 INT	17. 705.8 AME	18. VIDEO 020.321 HIL	19. VIDEO 314.2 WHI	20. VIDEO 509.22 DON

EXERCISE 8.5

1. 346.991 W587	2. 360 Y92	3. 363.25 G255	4. 363.25 G256	5. 363.25 L131
6. 363.25 M475	7. 364 B112	8. 364 H229	9. 364.021 D562	10. 364.099 A477
11. 364.0994 C929	12. 364.49 C928	13. 364.49 C929	14. 364.49 M476	15. 364.994 A198
16. 364.994 C297	17. 364.99402 C444	18. 364.994021 M953	19. 364.994021 W181	20. 364.994021 W182

EXERCISE 8.6

a.

1.	2.	3.	4.	5.
GN 324 .F531 1986	GN 325 .F47	GN 325 .F7 1979	GN 326 .F5 1989	GN 326 .F5 1991

b.

1.	2.	3.	4.	5.
Z699 .B53 D3 1986	Z699.5 .B5 D37 1985	Z699.5 .B53 D3 1984	Z699.5 .B53 D37 1983	Z699.5 .B53 D37 1987

c.

1.	2.	3.	4.	5.
PL42 .A552 M606 1993	PL282 .A5 M7 1942	PL2842 .A2 M61	PL2892 .A52 M6 1987	PL8224 .A502 M76 1990

d.

1.	2.	3.	4.	5.
BF575 .S75 K44	BF575 .9 .A86	GT4985 .N38	HJ2193 .F56	HJ2193 .S97
6.	7.	8.	9.	10.
HJ9931 .A44	HN850 .V5 A97	HN850 .Z9 V58	HV1 .C74	JA26 .A86
11.	12.	13.	14.	15.
JQ4011 .E49	Q1 .S34	QB1 .A89441	QB1 .R47	QB1 .5 .M67
16.	17.	18.	19.	20.
QB51 .A77	QB86 .S35	QL737 .C23 T475	TX717 .P43	TX724 .5 .B47

e.

1. DG5 .I61	2. DU967 .6 .K29	3. HM1 .A5	4. HM1 .A87	5. HM1 .5 .C72
6. HN850 .V5 A97	7. HN850 .Z9 V53	8. HN850 .Z9 V58	9. HQ1101 .W74	10. HV1 .C74
11. JA26 .A86	12. Q1 .R553	13. Q1 .R56	14. QB1 .5 .M67	15. QH540 .B75
16. QH540 .C3	17. QH540 .C38	18. QH540 .C4	19. SD1 .7 .W4	20. T1 .226 .U54

f.

1. DS611 .I44	2. HA31 .2 .M66	3. HD5345 .A6 C74	4. HT609 R43	5. HT609 .R5
6. HT609 .S33	7. HV9069 .C53	8. JV9185 .I8 C72	9. NC1115 .B7	10. PA2117 .A5
11. QA276 .8 .H34	12. QH508 .B3	13. QH508 .G7	14. QH511 .H35	15. QP33 .5 .C3
16. QP34 .L348	17. QP171 .S58	18. R127 .2 .V58	19. RC632 .P56 I57	20. S494 .5 .W3

REVISION QUIZ 8.8

1. In a closed access library, users do not have access to the shelves. Library staff collect materials from the closed stacks, which are often in accession order rather than classified by subject.

2. Some libraries shelve their materials in a fixed location because:
   - space is used more economically
   - the collection does not need to be respaced as often as it would in a relative location arrangement
   - there is less wear and tear on items.

3. Libraries use a classification scheme to shelve the materials by subject. Organized this way, the collection is browsable so that users can find related materials together on the shelves.

4. It is important to reshelve materials promptly to avoid the unnecessary effort involved in searching for "missing" items.

5.   The OH&S rules you must follow when shelving materials include:
        - Use a kick stool to reach the high shelves.
        - Sit on a kick stool when working on low shelves.
        - Pick up books with both hands.
        - Turn with your whole body including your feet.
        - Shelve for about three hours a day and vary tasks while shelving.
        - Switch hands periodically.
        - Load book trucks evenly because they can topple over easily when they are heavy.

EXERCISE 9.4

The client would be rather intimidated by the number of "do nots" in the rules. There is also the danger that the library might give the client some ideas on how to cause damage!

To improve these rules it would be better to use more positive comments such as "Please handle the books with care".

EXERCISE 9.5

Your guidelines should include comments on handling of material, loading of book trucks, correct ways to shelve materials, and how to handle material when making photocopies.

REVISION QUIZ 9.8

1.   A library prevents damage caused by people handling the materials by:
        - educating its users and staff in correct handling methods
        - restricting access to more valuable or fragile materials
        - substituting originals with copies.

2.   Here are the features of the ideal environment for preventing damage to library materials:
        - the lighting should be not too bright and not too dark
        - the relative humidity should be around 55%
        - the temperature should be around 70°F/21°C
        - air should circulate throughout the collection
        - it may be necessary to fumigate the library to destroy pests.

3.   It is important to repair damaged materials promptly to:
        - avoid further damage
        - ensure materials are returned to the shelves ready for use.

4.   When deciding whether an item is worth repairing, library staff need to consider the following factors:
        - Is the item needed immediately by a library user?
        - Does the library hold other copies of the item?
        - Is it possible to purchase a replacement?
        - Can the library afford to buy a replacement?
        - Is the item still in demand or only used infrequently?
        - How serious is the damage?
        - Does the library have the equipment and supplies needed to repair the damage?
        - Is the item out of date?
        - Is the information available in a different format?
        - Does the item belong to a special collection?
        - Is the item rare or valuable?

5. Libraries bind their serials to prolong their life and to keep issues together. Binding ensures that the issues stay in logical order and are protected from damage.

EXERCISE 10.1

Users find it frustrating to retrieve a record for an item and then find it is not available. Some online catalogs can mask records from the public display until the item is found or another copy is acquired. If the records are searchable in the catalog, the library might offer to acquire the material temporarily on interlibrary loan.

EXERCISE 10.2

1. If a library decided to weed all books that have not been borrowed in the last three years, it may discard some items that have been used in the library but not borrowed.

2. To stay up-to-date with changes in the curriculum, library staff need to communicate regularly with teaching staff.

3. Library staff decide whether a book is heavily used by looking at the loan records and also by examining its appearance.

4. The library decided to give preference to non-print formats of reference materials because they take up less space. Also, print formats are more likely to be damaged.

5. The library keeps only the most recent edition of reference books in the reference collection in order to save space and to allow users to borrow older editions that are shelved with the main collection.

6. Library staff check the physical condition of audiovisual materials by examining them closely and running their fingers along the sprocket holes of films to check for cracks. They might run the audiovisual materials on the appropriate equipment to check for damage.

7. The library consults the media department about the costeffectiveness of repairing audiovisual materials because they would have specialized knowledge on whether the materials can be repaired or whether they should be discarded.

8. The library checks to see whether another library holds a serial before cancelling a title to make sure that it is not the only library in an area which holds that title. If it is the only library, it might decide not to cancel the subscription.

9. The policy includes visual observation as a measure of serial use because some serials are used only in the library and are not available for loan; therefore the loan records cannot be used to measure use. Also, the physical appearance of the serial might be a determining factor in whether to retain or discard it.

REVISION QUIZ 10.3

1. Most libraries decide not to inventory the complete collection because of the effort involved. It is usually necessary to close the library, thus disrupting clients and other libraries.

2. A shelf list is a list of the library's holdings in the order in which they are arranged on the shelves.

3. It is important to shelf read the collection before doing inventory to ensure that all of the materials are in correct order. If the materials are out of order, staff take much longer conducting the inventory because they have to stop and reshelve items.

4. The reasons for weeding a library's collection include:
    - Material is worn out physically.
    - Availability of better materials.
    - The item has not been used or borrowed for a long time.
    - Community needs or the curriculum may have changed.
    - Institutional objectives may have changed, thereby changing the library's objectives.
    - Unwanted material can get in the way, resulting in crowded, untidy shelves that are awkward to use.
    - The costs of storage are too high.

5. Libraries are most likely to weed obsolete materials, superseded publications, and duplicate copies. They also weed unsolicited and unwanted donations, as well as materials that are too badly damaged to be worth repairing.

GLOSSARY

This glossary contains the main terms used in the book. For a comprehensive glossary, see Mortimer, Mary, *LibrarySpeak: a glossary of terms in librarianship and information management*, 4th ed. Canberra: DocMatrix, 2001.

AACR2 *See* Anglo-American Cataloguing Rules Second edition

academic library A library serving the information needs of the students and staff of a university or similar institution

access point A name, subject heading, title, or other element of a bibliographic description that is searchable in a library catalog

accession To record the particulars of each item as it is received in a library

acid-free paper Paper that is free of the acid that causes it to become yellowed and brittle over time

acquisitions The process of adding to a library's collection by purchase, gift, or exchange

added entry Any entry, other than the main entry and subject entries, by which the user can access the catalog (e.g., title, joint author, illustrator, editor, series, corporate body)

aggregator A company that acquires the distribution rights for different pieces of electronic information and packages it for sale to libraries and other information agencies

Anglo-American Cataloguing Rules Second edition (AACR2) Standardized rules for cataloging library materials, adopted by major libraries in most English-speaking countries and translated into many other languages. The rules are developed and copublished by the Library of Congress, the American Library Association, the Library Association (UK), and the Canadian Library Association

annual A serial published once a year

approval plan An arrangement between a library and a publisher or vendor for the selection and supply of all publications that match a pre-established collection profile (library has return privileges). *See also* blanket order

area of description A major section of the bibliographic description dealing with a particular category (e.g., publication details)

artifact An object made or modified by one or more persons

audiocassette An audiotape recording enclosed in a plastic case

audiovisual material Non-book materials such as audiocassettes, compact discs, slides, videotapes

author The person chiefly responsible for the intellectual or artistic content of a work (e.g., writer of a book, compiler of a bibliography, composer of a musical work, artist, photographer)

author entry An entry under the heading for an author as an access point, searchable in a library catalog

author number *See* book number

authority control The control of access points by establishing and using consistent headings

authority file A collection of authority records containing the preferred forms of headings for names, series, and subjects; can be on cards, microfiche, or online

authority record A record of the preferred heading for a person, place, corporate body, series, or title

back issue A noncurrent issue of a serial

back run A set of noncurrent issues of a serial

banning Forbidding client privileges such as borrowing, usually until fines are paid

barcode Product identification code made up of thick and thin lines; used to identify a library item uniquely

barcode reader/scanner A device used to read a barcode into a computer

bibliographic control The creation, organization, and management of records to describe items held in libraries or databases and to facilitate user access to those items

bibliographic description Description of an item by title, statement of responsibility, edition, publishing information, etc.

bibliographic instruction *See* library instruction

bibliographic record A description of an item in card, microtext, machine-readable, or other form containing sufficient information to identify the item; may include subject headings and call number

bibliography A list of related library materials or resources, usually subject-related

binding Adding a hard cover to a book or volume of serials

binding record A list of books and/or serials sent to the bindery

blanket order An arrangement between a library and a publisher or vendor to provide one copy of all publications in a particular category (library does not have return privileges). *See also* approval plan

book catalog A catalog printed and bound in book format

book jacket *See* dustjacket

book number The numbers, letters, or combination of numbers and letters used to distinguish an individual item from other items with the same classification number. *See also* Cutter number

bookcard A piece of cardboard or plastic that has the details of a particular book (e.g., author, title, call number); used when charging out a loan

borrower A library user who is entitled to check out materials

branch library A library other than the central library in a system

browse To examine a collection of library materials in an unsystematic way

BT Broader term; a more general subject heading

call number A number on a library item consisting of a classification number, a book number, and often a location symbol

card catalog A catalog composed of 7.5 x 12.5 cm. card entries filed in drawers

catalog A list of library materials contained in a collection, a library, or a group of libraries, arranged according to some definite plan

cataloger A person who prepares catalog entries and maintains a catalog so that library materials can be retrieved efficiently

cataloging The preparation of bibliographic information for catalog records; consists of descriptive cataloging, subject cataloging, and classification

cataloging tools Publications of the international cataloging rules and standards

charging Recording the loan of an item

check-in The process of recording the receipt of a specific issue of a serial

chronological designation Numbering of serials in date order (e.g., January 2001)

circulation Borrowing and returning of library items

circulation slip *See* routing slip

circulation system A system that stores and matches information on a library item with a borrower and the date due

claim A form or letter sent to a publisher or subscription agent notifying them of a serial issue that has not been received

classification number The number assigned to a library item to indicate a subject and to specify its location in the collection

classification scheme A particular scheme for arranging library materials according to subject (e.g., Dewey Decimal Classification, Library of Congress Classification)

classify To allocate a classification number

client A person who is served by a library or other information agency; also referred to as a borrower, patron, reader, etc.

client education *See* library instruction

closed access Where users only have access to items in the collection by requesting them from the library staff; most often occurs in large research libraries

collection development *See* selection

collection maintenance All the tasks required to maintain the library collection (e.g., shelving, weeding, repair)

compact disc A sound disc on which sound is recorded digitally and played back by laser

compiler A person who selects and puts together material written by other people or a person who writes a reference work made up of many different entries (e.g., a dictionary)

computer file A file of data encoded for processing by computer

copy cataloging The process of copying cataloging details from an existing catalog record and adding local location and holdings details

copyright The exclusive legal right granted by a government to an author, artist, composer, etc., to publish or sell their work within certain limitations

Cutter number A system of author numbers, devised by Charles A. Cutter, beginning with the first letter of the author's last name and followed by numbers; used in Library of Congress Classification for authors, titles, and geographic areas

Cutter-Sanborn number An extension of the Cutter author-number system, outlined in the Cutter-Sanborn Threefigure Tables; designed to maintain works with the same classification number in alphabetical order by author

database A collection of records in machine-readable format, each record being the required information about one item

date due The date on or before which materials should be returned to the library

date due slip A slip glued into a book that is used to record when it must be returned to the library

date of publication The earliest year in which the particular edition of the work was published (e.g., if a second edition was published in 1991 and reprinted without alteration in 1993, the date of publication of this edition remains 1991)

descriptive cataloging The process that describes an item, identifies and formats access points

Dewey Decimal Classification A classification scheme, devised by Melvil Dewey in 1873, using numbers to represent subjects

discharging Cancelling a loan record when an item is returned

distributor An agent with the marketing rights for an item

document delivery The delivery of published and unpublished information by conventional and electronic means, including electronic mail and facsimile transmission

download To transfer a file to one's own computer from another computer

dustjacket Paper cover for a hardcover book to protect the binding

edition All the copies of a work produced from the same original

edition statement The part of the description that indicates the particular edition of the work (e.g., revised, illustrated, student, abridged)

e-book A book either directly input into a computer or converted from print to electronic format, and made available via the Internet

e-journal A periodical published in electronic format and made available via the Internet

electronic publishing Making information available in electronic format, usually on the Internet

encumber The process of committing a certain sum of money to the payment of an order

endpapers The papers that join the front and back cover of a book to the central section

end processing *See* final processing

ephemera Material of current interest that is expected to be stored for a limited time (e.g., pamphlets, newspaper clippings)

exchange agreement A library trades material it owns with materials from another library; this arrangement is often used to exchange duplicate material

explanatory reference A longer "see" or "see also" reference that explains when a heading or headings should be used

extent of item Number and specific material designation of the parts of the item being described

field Unit of information in a MARC record that corresponds to an area of description or other piece of information (e.g., access point) or element of a record in a database

file as is File as the entry looks and not as it sounds (e.g., "Mr." is not filed as "Mister")

filing rules A set of rules for arranging records or cards in a file

final processing The preparation of an item, after it has been cataloged, for use in the library or for loan

fine A monetary penalty imposed on a user who returns library material after the due date

fixed location Arrangement of library materials in which items are shelved in a prescribed place and new items are added at the end of the sequence

format Appearance and makeup of a book (e.g., size, paper, type, binding, etc.), physical type of an audiovisual item (e.g., slide, filmstrip, etc.), or physical organization of a catalog (e.g., card, microfiche, online, etc.)

general material designation (GMD) Broad category of material to which an item belongs (e.g., microform, map)

hardcover Bound in cloth-covered or paper-covered boards

heading A name, word, or phrase used as an access point in a catalog

hold The status given to a library item in circulation and requested by another patron; the item can be put "on hold" for the next patron

holdings Collection of a library or information agency

ILL *See* interlibrary loan

index An alphabetical list of names, place, and/or subjects covered in a book, each followed by the page number(s) where it can be found in the text or a finding-guide to the literature of a specific field, usually in electronic format, searchable by topic, author, title, and keyword (e.g., *The Avery index to architectural periodicals*)

indicator Additional character used in some fields to provide extra information to the computer (e.g., the number of non-filing indicators)

information agency An organization that provides access to information (e.g., library, archive)

information technology The acquisition, processing, storage, and dissemination of information by means of computers and telecommunications

in print Available for purchase from the publisher

in-process file A file (manual or automated) of items received by a library and not yet available to users

integrated shelving Shelving in which all physical formats of material are shelved in one sequence

interlibrary loan (ILL) A loan made by one library to another for the use of an individual, including the provision of a photocopy of the original work requested

International Standard Bibliographic Description (ISBD) Standard set of bibliographic elements in standard order and with standard punctuation, published by the International Federation of Library Associations and Institutions (IFLA)

International Standard Book Number (ISBN) A unique ten-digit number assigned by R. R. Bowker in the United States and by the Canadian ISBN Agency in Canada. Identifies the publisher, language, and title

International Standard Serial Number (ISSN) A unique eight-digit number assigned by the International Serials Data System (ISDS) in the United States; Canadian publishers of serials can obtain ISSNs from ISSN Canada, a service of the National Library of Canada; identifies a specific serial publication

Internet A worldwide network of computer networks all linked together

intershelving *See* integrated shelving

inventory The checking of the contents of a library's collection against a list of the library's holdings. Usually done to identify how many items are missing, to meet audit requirements, and to assess the condition of the collection

invoice The document from the publisher or vendor requesting payment from the library for purchased items

ISBD *See* International Standard Bibliographic Description

ISBN *See* International Standard Book Number

ISSN *See* International Standard Serial Number

issue (n) A single copy of a serial title. (v) To lend an item

journal A periodical issued by an institution, corporation, or learned society containing current information and reports of activities or works in a particular field; also used as a synonym for periodical

Kardex® A specialized filing cabinet for storing serial check-in cards

large print Materials that are produced in larger than usual print (e.g., materials for the visually impaired and beginning readers, children's picture books)

letter-by-letter alphabetization Arranging in strict alphabetical order ignoring word breaks (e.g., Newbery before New England)

library A place housing a collection of materials for reading, study, reference, or from which to borrow or a collection of resources available in print and/or digital formats

Library of Congress The library of the United States Congress; the *de facto* national library of the United States

Library of Congress Classification A classification scheme developed by the Library of Congress using numbers and letters

Library of Congress Subject Headings The authoritative list of subject headings compiled and maintained by the Library of Congress

library instruction Teaching clients about library services, facilities, resources, and search strategies in order to help them derive the most benefit from using the library

library vendor A company whose primary function is to supply library materials from publishers

loan A recorded transaction in which a borrower removes an item from a collection for a stated period of time

location Where an item is housed; this can be the name of the library or the part of a collection

location symbol A symbol showing in which collection an item belongs (e.g., F for fiction)

magazine A popular periodical or a holder for slides to be shown using a slide projector; can also be used to store slides

main entry The principal entry in card and book catalogs; the entry with the fullest description of an item including the tracings

manuscript A handwritten or typescript document

map A representation, normally to scale, of an area of the earth's surface or another celestial body

MARC Machine readable cataloging; an internationally accepted standard developed by the Library of Congress in 1966 to enable libraries to share catalog records

material specific details Details that apply only to a particular material type such as the scale of a map

microfiche A microfilmed transparency about the size and shape of a filing card that can accommodate many pages of print

microfilm 16mm or 35mm wide film containing a sequence of microphotographs

microform Any form of microreproduction, including microfilm and microfiche, commonly used to preserve and store information in libraries because of its compact size

monograph A publication either complete in one part or in a finite number of separate parts

name authority file A collection of authority records containing the preferred forms of headings for personal and corporate names; can be on cards, microfiche, or online

national bibliography A listing of the publications of a country, about a country, and by the residents of a country

national library A library, funded by a national government, responsible for collecting and preserving the published, and perhaps the unpublished, heritage of the country

national union catalog A listing of the holdings of a large number of libraries in a country

network A system of physically separate computers with telecommunications links that allow the transfer of data among them

newspaper A printed publication issued regularly, usually daily or weekly, containing news, comment, features, and advertising

newspaper clipping/cutting An article cut from a newspaper; usually filed in a vertical file or photocopied and sent to identified library users

newsprint Paper on which newspapers are printed; contains a high proportion of ground wood pulp that causes the paper to become yellow and brittle when exposed to light

non-book material Material other than printed materials (e.g., audiovisual material, computer software)

notation In library classification, the symbols that stand for the classes, subclasses, divisions, and subdivisions of classes

numeric designation Numbering of a serial using numbers (e.g., volume 1, number 1)

on-demand publishing Allowing users to access a document or book (usually online) and then print or save it immediately, subject to copyright and likely for a fee

online public access catalog (OPAC) A library's computer-based catalog, often including other information such as special collections, patron information, and online services or databases; usually part of an integrated library system (ILS) allowing staff from different departments to share files

on-order file A listing of all the items ordered by a library and not yet received

OPAC *See* online public access catalog

open access Where users have direct access to items in the collection

orders complete file A listing of orders that have been processed; includes both cataloged items and cancelled orders

original cataloging Creating a bibliographic record for an item using cataloging tools

other title information Title on an item other than the title proper or parallel or series title; also any phrase appearing in conjunction with the title proper

overdue Kept beyond the due date

ownership mark/stamp A mark indicating which library owns a particular item; may be made with a rubber stamp or an embossing machine or may be handwritten

pagination The number of pages or leaves (or both) of a book identified in the bibliographic description of a book

pamphlet A small (usually less than fifty pages) printed work on a topic of current interest

pamphlet box A box usually made of cardboard, plastic, or metal that is used to store pamphlets and unbound serials

paperback A book bound in flexible heavy paper or cardboard covers

parallel title Title proper in another language and/or script found on the chief source of information

patron record The record in an electronic circulation system that includes information about a borrower (e.g., name, telephone number, items on loan, holds)

periodical A serial with a distinctive title intended to appear in successive parts at stated and regular intervals

physical description Information about the physical form of an item (e.g., pagination, type of recording, dimensions)

preservation Changing the state of library material in order to protect the content (e.g., microfilming newspapers, digitizing slides)

process To prepare an item for use in the library or for loan; involves adding an ownership stamp, tattle tape, call number label, etc.

public library A library funded by government that provides library services to all sections of the community

public services Services to library users including library instruction, meeting users' requests for specific information and assistance, and management of the use and loan of library material and equipment

publisher A person, firm, or corporate body responsible for producing a work in multiple copies and making it available for sale

purchase order An order placed with a supplier (e.g., government department or agency) that indicates a firm intention to purchase

realia Three-dimensional objects

recall (n) A request for the return from loan of a library item. (v) To request the return from loan of a library item

reciprocal borrowing The exchange of borrowing privileges between two libraries

record (n) A document or the data relating to a document (found in a catalog or database) (v) To preserve information in writing, typescript, or coded form or to reproduce sound and/or pictures using disc or magnetic tape

reference A direction from one heading or entry to another

reference collection A collection of books intended to be referred to rather than read; usually not for loan outside the library

relative location Library items shelved in relationship to others depending on the subject

renew To extend the period for which a library item is on loan

reserve collection A collection of material in high demand, usually in a teaching institution, with controlled access and shorter than normal loan periods

reshelve To replace items on the shelf in order

restricted loan *See* short loan

revision A new edition of a work containing alterations and/or additions

routing slip A list of users (e.g., faculty, staff) attached to a publication in the order in which the publication is to be routed

RT Related term; a subject heading at the same level of specificity to another heading and related in subject matter

scanner A device that converts images on paper to electronic impulses readable by a computer (e.g., barcode scanner, optical scanner)

school library A library in a school that offers library service to students and staff

search engine Computer software that retrieves documents based on words or phrases specified by a client; also the services—such as Altavista, Yahoo, Google—designed to enable clients to find information on the World Wide Web by typing keywords

security strip *See* tattle tape

see also reference A direction from one heading to another when both are used

see reference A direction from one heading, which is not used, to another heading that is used

segregated shelving The different formats of library materials are shelved separately according to their needs

selection The process of deciding which items to acquire for a library's collection

serial A publication issued in successive parts, often at regular intervals, and intended to be continued indefinitely

serial title The title of all issues of a serial; some serials also give titles to individual issues

serials control The process of managing the receipt, check-in, routing, and claiming of serials

series A number of works related to each other by the fact that they have a collective title, as well as each work having its own title

series title page An added title page providing the series title proper

shelf guide A sign to show the sequence of call numbers on a particular set of shelves

shelf list The record of the works in a library in the order in which they are shelved

shelf read To check the order of the materials on the shelves

shelve To place material in order on the shelves

short loan *See* reserve collection

silverfish Small insect that eats paper

slide A single frame of film, glass, or other transparent material mounted in cardboard or plastic; designed to be used with a projector or viewer

software Computer program that tells the computer what to do and how to do it

sound recording A generic term for a recording of sound; available in a number of formats that include audiocassette, phonograph or vinyl record, and compact disc (digital)

special collection A collection of materials that is treated in a special way because of its subject matter, age, value, etc.

special library A library specializing in a limited subject area. Usually maintained by a corporation, association, or government agency

spine label A label that is stuck on the spine of library materials to display the call number

standard number An ISBN, ISSN, or any other internationally agreed upon standard number that identifies the item uniquely

standardize Make standard by applying a set of rules

standing order An order for all future issues of a serial title or series of related items that is kept active until the publisher is notified that no more issues are required

statement of responsibility A statement taken from the item that describes the person(s) or corporate body responsible for the intellectual or artistic content of the item

subfield An element or subdivision of a field in a record

subject entry An entry under subject that is searchable in a library catalog

subject heading A heading that describes a subject of a work and provides subject access to a catalog

subscription An order for all issues of a periodical published within a certain time, usually one or two years; payment is made in advance for the whole period

subscription agent A person or company providing services to libraries wanting to purchase serials; the services include ordering subscriptions and standing orders, arranging payments and invoicing the library, following up missing issues, etc.

subtitles *See* other title information

supplements Extra and/or special issues of a serial title or materials issued separately that bring a monograph up to date or otherwise add to the work

supplier A company that sells equipment, furniture, and other supplies to libraries

tag The identifying label of a field in a record

tattle tape Magnetic tape inserted in a library item to activate an alarm if the item is removed from the library without being borrowed or checked out

technical services Library services that deal with the bibliographic control of library material (includes acquisitions, cataloging, and final processing)

telnet A protocol for access to text-only databases on the Internet, especially used for access to library catalogs

terms of availability Terms on which an item is available, including price or other statement

title entry An entry under title that is searchable in a library catalog

title page The page that provides the most complete information about the author and title and is used as the most authoritative source of cataloging data

title proper The main name of an item, including alternative title(s) but excluding parallel titles and other title information

tracings A record of the headings under which an item in entered in a catalog

trade bibliography A listing of books available for sale, together with details of publishers, etc., needed for purchase

typescript (adj) Written on a typewriter. (n) A typed manuscript

UF Used for; introduces nonpreferred headings; guides the cataloger to make a *see* reference from a term that is not used to one that is used

Uniform Resource Locator (URL) The address of a site on the World Wide Web

uniform title A title chosen to identify a monograph appearing under varying titles or a title used to distinguish the heading for one serial or series from the heading for another serial or series

union catalog Catalog describing the holdings of more than one library

verification Checking data to confirm bibliographic details before ordering

verso The back of a leaf of a book (e.g., verso of the title page); a left-hand page

vertical file A collection of ephemeral material including pamphlets and newspaper clippings; usually arranged in subject order in a filing cabinet

videotape Strip of mylar plastic tape covered with iron oxide that can be magnetized; sound and pictures are encoded as magnetic signals

vinyl record A sound disc made of vinyl plastic with sound grooves pressed into the surface

volume What is contained in one binding of a monograph or a number of issues of a serial, usually those published in one twelve-month period

weeding Discarding materials that are considered to be of no further use to the library

woodworm A worm or larva that is bred in or bores in wood

word-by-word alphabetization Arranging in strict alphabetical order within each word (e.g., New Town before newness)

World Wide Web (WWW) A networked information retrieval and communication environment; using hypertext transfer protocol (http) in the form of links (hyperlinks), computers connect documents and nontextual information such as graphics and sound files

Z39.50 A retrieval protocol often used in libraries to connect to other library catalogs and share bibliographic records

BIBLIOGRAPHY

Boucher, Virginia. *Interlibrary loan practices handbook.* Chicago, Ill.: American Library Association, 1996.

Evans, G. Edward, and Sandra M. Heft. *Introduction to technical services.* 6th ed. Englewood, Colo. : Libraries Unlimited, 1994.

Gosling, Mary, and Elizabeth Hopgood. *Learn about information.* 2nd ed. Canberra, Australia: DocMatrix, 2001.

Jeremy, Jenni. *Learn acquisitions and collection development.* Canberra, Australia: DocMatrix, forthcoming.

Mortimer, Mary. *Learn descriptive cataloging.* Lanham, Md.: Scarecrow Press & DocMatrix, 2000.

Protecting library materials from wear and tear. Madison, Wis.: Demco Video Productions, 1991.

Prytherch, Raymond John. *Harrod's librarians' glossary and reference book.* 9th ed. Aldershot, Hants., England: Gower, 2000.

Pymm, Bob. *Learn library management.* 2nd ed. Canberra, Australia: DocMatrix, 2000.

Schechter, Abraham A. *Basic book repair methods.* Englewood, Colo.: Libraries Unlimited, 1999.

Understanding the business of library acquisitions. Karen A. Schmidt, editor. Chicago, Ill.: American Library Association, 1999.

Internet Resources
Brodart's online *Book repair guide*
http://www.shopbrodart.com/onlineliterature/bookrepair/01bookrepair.htm

ODLIS: online dictionary of library and information science
http://www.wcsu.ctstateu.edu/library/odlis.html

National Interlibrary Loan Code for the United States
http://www.ala.org/rusa/stnd_lnc.html

Interlibrary Loan Information at the National Library of Canada
http://www.nlc-bnc.ca/ill/e-ill.htm

AcqWeb
http://acqweb.library.vanderbilt.edu/

INDEX

ABOUT THE AUTHORS

Elaine Andersen is a library educator at Canberra Institute of Technology in Canberra, Australia. She has worked in several special and public libraries and has taught a wide variety of subjects, including client services, acquisitions, and loan services, including interlibrary loan.

Mary Gosling is a reference librarian and library educator who has taught reference and basic library skills for many years. She is the author of *Learn Reference Work* and co-author of *Learn About Information* (both Scarecrow, forthcoming). Mary has been coordinator of the Library Studies Program at the Canberra Institute of Technology and is now a senior reference librarian at the National Library of Australia.

Trina Grover is the catalogue librarian at Ryerson University in Toronto. She has taught cataloging workshops and courses for Seneca College, continuing education at the Faculty of Information Studies at the University of Toronto, and for the Florida-based company The MARC of Quality.

Mary McConnell is head of bibliographic services at the University of Calgary Library. Mary has held a number of technical services positions at York University, Ryerson University, and the University of Regina. She also worked at the Faculty of Information Studies, University of Toronto, where she assisted in the research and design of a decision-making model for technical services and investigated the effectiveness of screen displays of online library catalogs.

Mary Mortimer is a teacher, librarian, author, and publisher. She is a director of DocMatrix Pty Limited and was coordinator of the Library Studies Program at the Canberra Institute of Technology in Canberra, Australia. She is the coauthor of *CatSkill* (InfoTrain, 1998), an interactive multimedia training program for libraries, author of *Learn Descriptive Cataloging* (Scarecrow, 2000) and *LibrarySpeak* (Scarecrow, forthcoming), and contributor to many other publications.